Second Edition

Strategic Reading 2

Jack C. Richards   Samuela Eckstut-Didier

CAMBRIDGE UNIVERSITY PRESS
Cambridge, New York, Melbourne, Madrid, Cape Town,
Singapore, São Paulo, Delhi, Mexico City

Cambridge University Press
32 Avenue of the Americas, New York, NY 10013-2473, USA

www.cambridge.org
Information on this title: www.cambridge.org/9780521281133

© Cambridge University Press 2012

First published 2012
2nd printing 2013

Printed in Hong Kong, China, by Golden Cup Printing Company Limited

A catalog record for this publication is available from the British Library.

ISBN 978-0-521-28113-3 Student's Book
ISBN 978-0-521-28115-7 Teacher's Manual

Book design: TSI Graphics
Layout services: Page Designs International, Inc.
Photo research: TSI Graphics

Contents

Scope and Sequence

Unit	Readings	Reading Strategies
Unit 1 **Names**	1 What's Your Name? 2 Do People Like Their Names? 3 The Right Name	Making Inferences Organizing Information into a Chart Predicting Recognizing Point of View Scanning Skimming Thinking About the Topic
Unit 2 **Helping Others**	1 Don't Just Stand There 2 Random Acts of Kindness 3 Monkey Business	Identifying Supporting Details Predicting Skimming Summarizing Thinking About the Topic Visualizing Information in a Text
Unit 3 **Movies**	1 A Dangerous Career in the Movies 2 Life as a Movie Extra 3 The Storyteller	Identifying Supporting Details Making Inferences Predicting Skimming Thinking About What You Know Thinking Beyond the Text
Unit 4 **Families**	1 Living with Mother 2 Father's Day 3 The Sandwich Generation	Identifying Supporting Details Making Inferences Previewing Vocabulary Scanning Skimming Thinking About the Topic Thinking About What You Know Visualizing Information in a Text
Unit 5 **Men and Women**	1 The Knight in Shining Armor 2 Men, Women, and TV Sports 3 Boys and Girls in Class	Making Inferences Predicting Recognizing Contrast in a Text Recognizing Purpose Skimming Thinking About the Topic
Unit 6 **Communication**	1 Spotting Communication Problems 2 Watch Your Language! 3 What Is Text Messaging Doing to Us?	Paraphrasing Predicting Recognizing Purpose Skimming Thinking About the Topic Thinking About What You Know Understanding Reference Words and Phrases

Introduction

Overview

Strategic Reading is a three-level series for young adult and adult learners of English. As its title suggests, the series is designed to develop strategies for reading, vocabulary-building, and critical thinking skills. Each level features texts from a variety of authentic sources, including newspapers, magazines, books, and Web sites. The series encourages students to examine important topics in their lives as they build essential reading skills.

The second level in the series, *Strategic Reading 2*, is aimed at high-intermediate level students. It contains 12 units divided into three readings on popular themes such as names, movies, dishonesty, and the senses. The readings in *Strategic Reading 2* range in length from 400 to 550 words and are accompanied by a full range of activities.

The units (and the readings within units) can be taught either in the order they appear or out of sequence. The readings and exercises, however, increase in difficulty throughout the book.

The Unit Structure

Each unit has the same ten-page structure. It includes a one-page unit preview and three readings, each of which is accompanied by two pre-reading tasks and four post-reading tasks.

Unit Preview
Each unit begins with a brief summary of the three readings in the unit. These summaries are followed by questions that stimulate students' interest in the readings and allow them to share their knowledge of the topic.

Pre-Reading Tasks
Each reading is accompanied by two pre-reading tasks: a reading preview task and a skimming or scanning task.

Reading Preview
Before each reading, students complete one of four types of pre-reading exercises: *Predicting*, *Previewing Vocabulary*, *Thinking About the Topic*, or *Thinking About What You Know*. These exercises prepare students to read and help them connect the topic of the reading to their own lives. Students identify information they expect to read, learn new vocabulary, write down what they know about the topic, or mark statements that are true about themselves.

Skimming/Scanning

One *Skimming* or *Scanning* exercise accompanies every reading. Before reading the whole text, students learn either to scan a text to look for specific information or to skim a text to get the gist. Other activities in this section ask students to confirm predictions from the reading preview section, compare their experiences with the writer's experiences, or identify the writer's opinion.

Post-Reading Tasks

Following each reading, there are four post-reading tasks: A–D. These tasks respectively check students' comprehension, build their vocabulary, develop a reading strategy, and provide an opportunity for discussion.

A Comprehension Check

The task immediately following the reading is designed to check students' comprehension. In some cases, students check their understanding of the main ideas. In others, students have to delve more deeply into the text for more detailed information.

B Vocabulary Study

This section is designed to help students understand six to eight words that appear in the text. Students use contextual clues, recognize similarity in meaning between words, or categorize words according to meaning.

C Reading Strategy

An important part of *Strategic Reading* is reading strategy development. Students are introduced to a variety of strategies, such as making inferences, summarizing, and understanding pronoun reference. (For a full list of reading strategies, see the Scope and Sequence on pages iv-v.) Practicing these strategies will help students gain a deeper understanding of the content of the text and develop the necessary strategies they will need to employ when they read on their own outside of the classroom. The section opens with a brief explanation of the reading strategy and why it is important.

D Relating Reading to Personal Experience

This section asks three open-ended questions that are closely connected to the topic of the reading. It gives students an opportunity to share their thoughts, opinions, and experiences in discussion or in writing. It is also a chance to review and use vocabulary introduced in the text.

Timed Reading

Each unit ends with an invitation for students to a timed reading task. Students are instructed to reread one of the texts in the unit, presumably the one they understand best, and to time themselves as they read. They then record their time in the chart on page 124 so that they can check their progress as they proceed through the book. (Naturally, there is no harm in students rereading and timing themselves on every text in a unit. However, this could be de-motivating for all but the most ambitious of students.)

Reading Strategies

Reading is a process that involves interaction between a reader and a text. A successful reader is a strategic reader who adjusts his or her approach to a text by considering questions such as the following:

- What is my purpose in reading this text? Am I reading it for pleasure? Am I reading it to keep up-to-date on current events? Will I need this information later (on a test, for example)?

- What kind of text is this? Is it an advertisement, a poem, a news article, or some other kind of text?

- What is the writer's purpose? Is it to persuade, to entertain, or to inform the reader?

- What kind of information do I expect to find in the text?

- What do I already know about texts of this kind? How are they usually organized?

- How should I read this text? Should I read it to find specific information or should I look for the main ideas? Should I read it again carefully to focus on the details?

- What linguistic difficulties does the text pose? How can I deal with unfamiliar vocabulary, complex sentences, and lengthy sentences and paragraphs?

- What is my opinion about the content of the text?

Reading strategies are the decisions readers make in response to questions like these. They may prompt the reader to make predictions about the content and organization of a text based on background knowledge of the topic as well as familiarity with the text type. They may help the reader decide the rate at which to read the text – a quick skim for main ideas, a scan for specific information, a slower, closer reading for more detailed comprehension, or a rapid reading to build fluency. Other reading strategies help the reader make sense of the relationships among the ideas, such as cause and effect, contrast, and so on. In addition, the strategy of reading a text critically – reacting to it and formulating opinions about the content – is a crucial part of being a successful reader.

The *Strategic Reading* series develops fluency and confidence in reading by developing the student's repertoire of reading strategies. Students learn how to approach a text, how to choose appropriate strategies for reading a text, how to think critically about what they read, and how to deal with the difficulties that different kinds of texts may pose.

Jack C. Richards

Authors' Acknowledgments

We would like to thank Bernard Seal for his efforts in getting the project going, for his vision in setting the second edition down a new path, and for his insightful comments until the very end.

We are also grateful to the production and design staff that worked on this new edition of *Strategic Reading*: our in-house editors, Alan Kaplan, Brigit Dermott, and Chris Kachmar; TSI Graphics; and Don Williams, who did the composition.

For their useful comments and suggestions, many thanks to the reviewers: Laurie Blackburn, Cleveland High School, Seattle, Washington; Alain Gallie, Interactive College of Technology, Atlanta, Georgia; John Howrey, Nanzan University, Nagoya, Japan; Ana Morales de Leon, Instituto Tecnologico de Monterrey, Monterrey, Mexico; Sheryl Meyer, American Language Institute, University of Denver, Denver, Colorado; Donna Murphy-Tovalin, Lone Star College, Houston, Texas; Richard Patterson, King Saud University, Saudi Arabia; Byongchul Seo, Yonsei University, Seoul, South Korea.

Finally, a writer is nobody without a good editor. In that vein, we are grateful to Amy Cooper and Kathleen O'Reilly for their critical eye and their expert guidance. And to Amy Cooper in her role as project manager, we owe many thanks for her patience, understanding, and good sense of humor.

Jack C. Richards
Sydney, Australia

Sammi Eckstut
Melrose, Massachusetts, USA

UNIT 1 Names

Look at the titles of the readings and their brief descriptions to preview this unit's content. Before you begin each reading, answer the questions about it.

Reading 1

What's Your Name?

Naming traditions are not the same all over the world. This article looks at several different traditions and shows how they can create problems for computer databases.

1. How many names do you have? One? Two? Three? More?

2. Do your friends and your parents call you by the same name? How do other people address you?

3. How did your parents choose your name?

Reading 2

Do People Like Their Names?

This newspaper article discusses why names are so important to us.

1. Do you have a common name, or do you have an unusual name?

2. Do you like your name? Have you always liked it?

3. Do you have a nickname? If so, what is it? Do you prefer your nickname to your real name?

Delana

Reading 3

The Right Name

Google   Nike   PepsiCo   Xerox   Yahoo

What decisions are involved in choosing the right name for a business? Find out the history behind the names of five well-known companies.

1. When you think of products with catchy names, which come to mind?

2. What are the names of three popular Web sites on the Internet? Do you think they have catchy names?

3. What qualities does a good brand name have?

What's Your Name?

Predicting

You are going to read about naming traditions in different cultures. Work with a partner. Check (✓) the statements you think the writer says are true.

_____ 1. In English-speaking countries, everyone has a first name, a middle name, and a last name.

_____ 2. Most people in Spanish-speaking countries have one family name.

_____ 3. In some Asian countries, the family name comes before the given, or first, name.

_____ 4. In Iceland, a brother and sister have different last names.

_____ 5. Today, international names are not a problem for computer databases.

Skimming

Skim the reading to check your answers. Then read the whole text.

1   Do you ever have problems when you fill out an electronic form because it is difficult to enter your name correctly? Most forms in English-speaking countries ask for your first name, sometimes a middle name or initial, and your last name. A first name is sometimes called a given name. It refers to the name that identifies you as an individual. It's the name used by your family and friends. "Last name" is your family name, that is, the name you share with your parents, siblings, and sometimes other members of your family. Many people in English-speaking countries also have a middle name. But this pattern – first, middle, last – isn't always appropriate for names in other languages.

2   In Spanish and Portuguese, it's common for single people to use their first name followed by their father's and then their mother's last names. Sometimes _de_[1] precedes the

_____
[1] _de:_ "of" in Spanish

mother's last name. For example, Maria-Jose Carreño Quiñones might be the daughter of Antonio Carreño Rodríguez and Anna Quiñones Marqués. If she includes *de*, she would be Maria-Jose Carreño de Quiñones. You would refer to her as Señorita[2] Carreño, not Señorita Quiñones.

In some Asian countries, people usually write their family name first, followed by their given name. For example, in the Chinese name Yao Ming, *Yao* is the family name and *Ming* is the given name. If he is in an English-speaking country, Yao Ming may replace his given name with an English name, for example, Fred. His English name would then be Fred Yao. 3

In the Icelandic name Björk Jónsdóttir, Björk is the given name. The second part of the name indicates the father's (or sometimes the mother's) name, followed by *-sson* for a male and *-sdóttir* for a female. Björk's father, Jón, was the son of Gunnar, and he is called Jón Gunnarsson. Icelanders prefer to be called by their given name (Björk) or their full name (Björk Jónsdóttir). In fact, in Iceland, telephone directories are sorted by given names. To avoid confusion, people's professions appear next to their names. 4

So how would Maria-Jose Carreño de Quiñones fill out a form that asks for first name, middle name or initial, and last name? Should she write Carreño or Quiñones as her last name? Will a database recognize the hyphen between the first and last parts of her first name? If Yao Ming writes his name in that order, he will be addressed as Mr. Ming, but "Ming" is actually his first, or given, name. If you were addressing Björk Jónsdóttir, she would be surprised if you called her Ms. Jónsdóttir. 5

Electronic forms also have trouble with apostrophes or capital letters in the middle of a name. For example, the Irish name O'Reilly may print out as "Oreilly" or "O. Reilly." And the Scottish name McAlister may print as "Mc Alister" or "Mcalister." 6

These are just a few of the problems that software designers encounter and are trying to solve. Today, the only truly useful electronic form or database is one that is able to accommodate international names. 7

---

[2] *Señorita:* "Miss" in Spanish

A Comprehension Check

Circle the letter of the correct answer.

1. What do you know about Anna Quiñones Marqués?
   a. Her father's last name is Marqués.
   b. Her mother's last name is Quiñones.
   c. Her mother's last name is Marqués.
   d. Her husband's last name is Quiñones.

2. Yao Ming's father's first name is Zhiyuan. What is his father's full name?
   a. Zhiyuan Ming
   b. Ming Zhiyuan
   c. Yao Ming Zhiyuan
   d. Yao Zhiyuan

3. Björk Jónsdóttir is married to Stefán Magnússon. What is the most probable choice for the name of their daughter Unnur?
   a. Unnur Jónsdóttir
   b. Unnur Magnússon
   c. Unnur Magnússdóttir
   d. Unnur Stefánsdóttir

B Vocabulary Study

Find the words in the box in the reading. Then complete the sentences.

fill out (par. 1)	enter (par. 1)	siblings (par. 1)
precedes (par. 2)	indicates (par. 4)	accommodate (par. 7)

1. I have two _____. My brother's name is Harris, and my sister's name is Rebecca.

2. In the English alphabet, the letter *Y* _____ the letter *Z*.

3. All new employees have to _____ this form.

4. Then the company can _____ your personal information into its database.

5. We can't _____ everyone. We have space for only 100 people.

6. An initial between a first and last name _____ that the person has a middle name.

C Recognizing Point of View

Sometimes a writer expresses a point of view, or an opinion. An important part of reading critically is the ability to recognize if the writer has expressed a point of view and if so, to understand what that point of view is.

Check (✓) the statement that best expresses the writer's point of view.

_____ 1. People should learn about naming traditions in other countries.

_____ 2. Things would be simpler if there weren't different naming traditions.

_____ 3. Electronic databases make it easy for people to enter their names correctly.

_____ 4. Electronic databases need to be improved so that they can deal with names from all over the world.

D Relating Reading to Personal Experience

Discuss these questions with your classmates.

1. How would your name be different if you were in one of the parts of the world mentioned in the reading?

2. How would you explain the naming traditions of your culture to someone from a different culture?

3. Do people ever change their names in your culture? If so, when is it common to change names?

Do People Like Their Names?

Ember

Delana

Thinking About the Topic

**Check (✓) the statements that are true for you.
Compare your answers with a partner.**

_____ 1. I'm glad I have a nickname.

_____ 2. I like my name because it is original.

_____ 3. I like my name now. But when I was a child, my name bothered me because it is unusual.

_____ 4. I'm not sure I like my name.

_____ 5. Sometimes people mispronounce my name.

Skimming

Skim the reading to see which statements are true for Delana and which are true for Ember. Write _D_ or _E_ next to each statement. Then read the whole text.

As a shy girl growing up, Delana Pence got a lot of teasing from other children. Her 1
unusual first name didn't help matters. "People would mispronounce it or make fun of it,"
said Pence. "I asked myself why my parents named me this. Why couldn't I be a Cindy or
a Rhonda?" Life got easier in junior high school when someone – Pence can't remember
who – started calling her Dee, and the nickname stuck. "I have been called Dee ever

since, except by my family, who has always called me Delana." In time, Pence came to terms with her name. "It's a pretty name, but it took me all these years to struggle with it and figure that out," she said.

2   Her change of heart doesn't surprise Cleveland Kent Evans, an associate professor of psychology at Bellevue University, who has studied given names for more than 30 years. "A great many people – more women than men – go through a period during their adolescence where they dislike their names as part of the general adolescent concern with identity and what other people think of them," he said. "But I think for most people these feelings subside by the time they are in their 30s." Most people, Evans and other psychologists say, go through life with a favorable view of their names.

3   What is it about names that makes them important, anyway? Why do they matter? In the book *The Language of Names*, Justin Kaplan and Anne Bernays try to answer such questions. "Names penetrate the core of our being and are a form of poetry, storytelling, magic, and compressed history," the authors write. "Apparently there has never been a society able to get along without them. They are among the first things we ask or learn when we meet someone new, and we use them to form immediate but often unreliable conclusions about personality and ethnicity." Names define us. "They're the anchor around which we build our identity," Evans said. "When you think of yourself, the first thing you think of is your name."

4   Ember Gibson, a student, seems to be struggling with an identity issue. She is unsure about how she feels about her name. "I get teased often, but then I have people compliment me, too," Ember said. "Most of the kids call me Amber. Some say, 'Are you on fire?' And others say, 'What?' When I stop and think about it, though, I like that it's original. . . . Maybe by the time I graduate, I'll know if I like it or not."

Adapted from *The Columbus Dispatch*

A Comprehension Check

Every paragraph in the reading is about one topic. Write the correct paragraph number for each topic.

_____ a. This paragraph discusses why names are so important to people.

_____ b. This paragraph explains why one person is not sure whether or not she likes her name.

_____ c. This paragraph describes how one person's feelings have changed over a period of time.

_____ d. This paragraph explains that most adults like their names, despite how they felt when they were younger.

B Vocabulary Study

Find the words and phrases in *italics* in the reading. Then match the words and phrases with their meanings.

_____ 1. *stuck* (par. 1)

_____ 2. *came to terms with* (par. 1)

_____ 3. *change of heart* (par. 2)

_____ 4. *subside* (par. 2)

_____ 5. *favorable* (par. 2)

_____ 6. *core* (par. 3)

_____ 7. *teased* (par. 4)

a. the most important part

b. become less and less

c. different opinion

d. accepted a difficult situation

e. laughed at

f. continued or stayed

g. positive

C Making Inferences

> Sometimes the reader must infer, or figure out, what the writer did not explain or state directly in the text.

Check (✓) the statements that you can infer from the reading.

_____ 1. Delana didn't know why her parents chose her name.

_____ 2. Cindy and Rhonda are common names.

_____ 3. Delana's family prefers her real name to her nickname.

_____ 4. Adolescent males like their names.

_____ 5. Names were important in ancient societies.

_____ 6. Amber is a more common name than Ember.

_____ 7. Ember will like her name when she's an adult.

D Relating Reading to Personal Experience

Discuss these questions with your classmates.

1. If you have children, what will you name them? Why? If you already have children, what names did you choose? Why?

2. What are your three favorite English names for males? For females?

3. If you could change your name, what would you change it to? Why?

The Right Name

Thinking About the Topic

Look at the names of these companies. Which companies do you think have good or memorable names? Do you know how the companies got those names? Discuss your answers with a partner.

Google   Nike   PepsiCo   Xerox   Yahoo

Scanning

Scan the reading to find and circle the company names. Find out the original names of these companies. Then read the whole text.

1   What is a six-letter word that immediately comes to mind when you need some information on the Internet? You probably thought of Google. But Google wasn't always the name of the famous search engine. In fact, the original name was BackRub!

2   BackRub was the name two graduate students gave to the new search engine they developed in 1996. They called it BackRub because the engine used backlinks[1] to measure the popularity of Web sites. Later, they wanted a better name – a name that suggests huge quantities of data. They thought of the word *googol*. (A googol is a number followed by 100 zeros.) When they checked the Internet registry of names to see if *googol* was already taken, one of the students misspelled the word by mistake, and that's how Google was born.

---

[1] *backlink:* If you publish a Web page, other people's links to your site are called backlinks.

Google is just one example of a name change in the business world. Many other companies have decided to change their names or the names of their products. Their reasons are usually different, but the goal is always the same: to find a name that is unique, easy to pronounce, and easy to remember.

Here are some more examples:

Jerry Yang and David Filo, two young computer specialists, developed a guide to Internet content in 1994. They called it "Jerry and David's Guide to the World Wide Web." But they soon realized that this wasn't a very catchy name, so they searched through a dictionary and found a better one: "Yahoo."

Sometimes companies change their names because of the popularity of one of their products. The Xerox Corporation is a good example. Xerox has been a familiar name in workplaces and schools for many years, but the company wasn't always called Xerox. Its original name was the Haloid Company, and it produced photographic paper. In 1947, the company developed a photocopy machine based on a technique known as xerography. The photocopiers became so well known that Haloid decided to change its name to Xerox in 1961.

A similar situation occurred in the world of athletic sportswear. In 1962, a young runner named Phil Knight started a company called Blue Ribbon Sports. He wanted to distribute Japanese running shoes, called Tigers, to the United States. In 1971, Knight decided to design and manufacture his own brand of shoes. He named the shoes after the Greek goddess of victory – Nike. Nike shoes became so well known that Knight changed the name of the whole company to Nike.

Name changes in business go back many years. Consider "Brad's Drink." This was the name of a soft drink invented by an American pharmacist, Caleb Bradham, in 1893. Bradham discovered a new way to make a sweet, fizzy cola drink. He decided that a better name would help sell the product worldwide. He called both the drink and his company Pepsi-Cola. Some people believe that this name was based on two ingredients in the drink – pepsin and cola nuts. Today Pepsi-Cola is one of the most popular soft drinks, and the company's current name, PepsiCo, is famous around the world.

A Comprehension Check

Complete the statements with *Google, Yahoo, Xerox, Nike,* or *PepsiCo.*

1. Before it became the official name of a company, the name _____ was well-known in offices and schools.

2. The name _____ is not related to its product, and it's much shorter than the original name.

3. The original company name of _____ came from two ingredients in a drink.

4. Both _____ and _____ changed the names of their companies to the names of their most popular products.

5. _____ got its name from a word for a number.

B Vocabulary Study

Find the words and phrases in *italics* in the reading. Then circle the correct meanings.

1. If a name *suggests* something, it **makes you think of / describes** something. (par. 2)

2. If you *misspelled* a word, you **didn't spell / spelled** it correctly. (par. 2)

3. If you do something *by mistake*, you do it **accidentally / without any errors**. (par. 2)

4. When you *distribute* a product, you **make it available / stop selling it**. (par. 6)

5. When you are *named after* someone, you have **a different / a similar or the same** name. (par. 6)

6. A *fizzy* drink has **bubbles / sugar**. (par. 7)

C Organizing Information into a Chart

> Organizing information into a chart can help you deepen your understanding of a reading and see how different parts of the reading relate to each other.

Complete the chart with information about each company.

Name of company	Person(s) who started company	Original name of company	Origin of current name of company
Google			
Yahoo			*a catchy word in the dictionary*
Xerox			
Nike			
PepsiCo			

D Relating Reading to Personal Experience

Discuss these questions with your classmates.

1. How important is the name of a product to its success? For example, if Google had never changed its name from BackRub, would it be as popular as it is today?

2. Name three products that are not mentioned in the reading. Are the names of the products unique, easy to pronounce, and easy to remember? Which product has the best name?

3. Make up a name for a new product. Can your classmates guess what the product is?

> Reread one of the unit readings and time yourself. Note your reading speed in the chart on page 124.

2 Helping Others

Look at the titles of the readings and their brief descriptions to preview this unit's content. Before you begin each reading, answer the questions about it.

Reading 1 ▶ ## Don't Just Stand There

In this magazine article, the writer discusses how people typically react in emergency situations.

1. What would you do if someone suddenly collapsed on the sidewalk in front of you?

2. Do you think most people would take action in an emergency? Why or why not?

3. Have you ever been a bystander at an accident? If so, what did you do?

Reading 2 ▶ ## Random Acts of Kindness

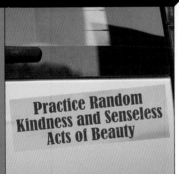

Are we as kind as possible to other people? What else could we do? This article from the Internet offers some suggestions.

1. When was the last time someone was very kind to you? What did they do or say?

2. Are most people likely to do kind things for strangers? Why or why not?

3. If you do nice things for other people, do you think that might make them act more kindly toward others? Explain your answer.

Reading 3 ▶ ## Monkey Business

This newspaper article explains how a trained monkey helps a paralyzed person.

1. What kind of help do people with serious physical disabilities need at home?

2. What do you think an animal could do to help a disabled person?

3. Do you think an animal can lift a person's spirits? If so, how?

Don't Just Stand There

Thinking About the Topic

Check (✓) the reasons why you might *not* help other people in trouble. Compare your answers with a partner.

_____ 1. You don't want to get involved.

_____ 2. You don't feel competent.

_____ 3. You're not sure help is needed.

_____ 4. You're in too much of a hurry.

_____ 5. You think that someone else will help.

_____ 6. Other people don't look concerned.

Skimming

Skim the reading to find and circle the reasons the writer includes. Then read the whole text.

1   You're rushing to work and a man ahead of you collapses on the sidewalk. Do you stop to help? In a study of bystanders, it was found that some people look away or keep on walking rather than stop and get involved.

2   "There is an inclination to decide that no action is needed," says Ervin Staub, a psychologist at the University of Massachusetts at Amherst, who studies the role of bystanders. "The first thoughts that come into your mind often keep you from offering help." Common thoughts that might prevent you from helping include:

   ◆ *Why should I be the one to help? I'm probably not the most competent person in this crowd.* You might think someone older or with more medical knowledge should offer assistance.

   ◆ *What if the person doesn't really need my help?* You don't want to be embarrassed. The fear of embarrassment is powerful; no one wants to risk looking foolish in front of others.

♦ **No one else looks concerned – this must not be a problem.** We take social cues from the people around us – but most people tend to hold back their emotions in public.

Time and again, good and caring people fail to come to the aid of others. They know they should act and yet, for reasons they themselves don't understand, people sometimes don't respond. Longtime researchers of bystander behavior continue to struggle with the question, "Why"?   3

Social psychologist Michael White says that it's easy to say that our society is becoming more violent and less sensitive. "But," he continues, "when you talk to people who observe these situations, they are usually very upset."   4

One thing we do know is that the more ambiguous a situation, the less likely people are to help. Let's say you see vapors coming out of a building. You ask yourself, "Is it steam or smoke?" If you are not sure, you look to other people for a clue about how to react. If you see other people are doing nothing, you think, "Of course, that's just steam." You don't want it to be smoke, because then you would have to do something about it.   5

Another well-known deterrent to action is known as "the bystander effect." This says that the more people there are observing an emergency, the less responsible each one of them personally feels. For example, if you are the only person in the world who can act to save someone in a dangerous situation, you are more likely to act. However, if you are one of 100,000 people who could save the situation, you would be happier if one of the other 99,999 people did it!   6

"If you spot trouble and find yourself rationalizing inaction, force yourself to stop and evaluate the situation instead of walking on," says Ervin Staub. Then try to involve other people; you don't have to take on the entire responsibility of being helpful. According to Staub, it is sometimes just a matter of turning to the person next to you and saying, "It looks like we should do something." Once you take action, most people will take their cues from you and also help.   7

Adapted from *Glamour* and *McCall's*

A Comprehension Check

Write the number of the paragraph where you can find the following information.

_____ a. suggestions of ways to take action when someone needs help

_____ b. the thoughts that often stop people from helping others

_____ c. why people who are part of a crowd often don't act

_____ d. the difficulty of understanding why most people don't offer to help in an emergency

_____ e. what people do when they're not sure about what is happening

_____ f. the results of a study of people in emergency situations

_____ g. how people feel when they see an emergency

B Vocabulary Study

Find the words in the box in the reading. Then complete the sentences.

inclination (par. 2)	assistance (par. 2)	cues (par. 2 & 7)
sensitive (par. 4)	ambiguous (par. 5)	deterrent (par. 6)

1. A good _____ against crime is to lock all your doors and windows.

2. They are not _____ to the problems of others. They just don't care.

3. His response to our dinner invitation was _____. It wasn't clear if he wanted to come or not.

4. If you visit another country and are not sure how to behave, take your _____ from the people who live there.

5. When his car wouldn't start, he asked his neighbor for _____.

6. Jane always had a strong _____ to help others, so she became a doctor.

C Identifying Supporting Details

> Supporting details in a text explain the main ideas more fully. If you can identify supporting details, you will have a clearer understanding of the writer's main ideas.

Look back at the reading and find details to support these main ideas.

1. *The first thoughts that come into your mind often keep you from offering help.* (par. 2)

   a. _____

   b. _____

   c. _____

2. *They know they should act and yet . . . people sometimes don't respond. "Why"?* (par. 5 & 6)

   a. _____

   b. _____

D Relating Reading to Personal Experience

Discuss these questions with your classmates.

1. Are people in your culture likely to help others in emergencies? Why or why not?

2. What do you think is the best thing to do in each of the following situations?
   a. Some teenagers are trying to grab a woman's purse.
   b. Someone is screaming outside your window in the middle of the night.
   c. A student next to you suddenly becomes ill during an important exam.

3. Have you or a friend ever needed help in an emergency? If so, what happened?

Practice Random
Kindness and Senseless
Acts of Beauty

Random Acts of Kindness

Predicting

Look at the title. What does *random* mean? Look up the word in a dictionary if necessary. Then check (✓) the statement that best explains the meaning of the sentence: "Practice random acts of kindness." Compare your answers with a partner.

_____ 1. Do kind things for strangers from time to time.

_____ 2. Be nice to your friends and compliment them.

_____ 3. Don't think so much about yourself and your own needs.

Skimming

Skim the reading to check your prediction. Then read the whole text.

On a cold winter day in San Francisco, a woman drives up to the Bay Bridge tollbooth. 1
"I'm paying for myself, and for the six cars behind me," she says with a smile. One after another, the next six drivers arrive at the tollbooth, money in hand, only to be told: "Some lady up ahead already paid your toll for you. Have a nice day."

It turned out the woman had read something a friend had taped to her refrigerator: 2
"Practice random kindness and senseless[1] acts of beauty." She liked the idea so much she copied it down.

Judy Foreman spotted the same words painted on a wall a hundred miles from her 3
home. They stayed on her mind for days, so she wrote them down. "I thought the idea was incredibly beautiful," she said, explaining why she now puts it at the bottom of all the letters she writes.

Her husband Frank liked the idea so much that he put it up on the wall for his 4
students, one of whom was the daughter of a local newspaper journalist. The journalist put it in the newspaper, even though she wasn't sure what it really meant.

[1] In this context, *senseless* means unnecessary.

5   A woman named Anne Herbert from Marin, California, saw the words in the newspaper. She thought about them for days, and one day in a restaurant wrote them down on her placemat. A man sitting near her looked over her shoulder and saw what she had written. "That's wonderful," he said, and he copied the words down on his own placemat.

6   "Here's the idea," Herbert told the man. "Anything you think there should be more of, do it randomly." Her own ideas include going into schools in poor neighborhoods to paint the classrooms, preparing hot meals for the hungry, and putting some money into a needy woman's hand. Herbert believes that kindness can build on itself, just as much as violence can. Now the idea is spreading, on car bumper stickers, on walls, at the bottom of letters and business cards. And as it spreads, so do people's ideas about the kind things they can do for others.

7   In Portland, Oregon, a man puts a coin into a stranger's parking meter just in time. In Patterson, New Jersey, a dozen people with pails, mops, and flower seeds go to a house in bad condition and clean it while the elderly owners look on, surprised and smiling. A man in St. Louis, whose car has just been hit by a young woman, smiles and says, "It's a scratch. Don't worry."

8   Random acts of beautification spread, too. A man plants flowers along the roadway. In Seattle, another man decides that he's going to clean up the trash people have left on city streets. In Atlanta, a man removes graffiti from a park bench.

9   You can't smile without making yourself feel happier. And you can't carry out a random act of kindness without feeling as if your own troubles have become less important. If you were one of those drivers who found your bridge toll paid, who knows what you might do for someone else later? Wave someone to go on ahead of you when your car comes to an intersection? Smile at a tired clerk? Kindness begins slowly with a single act. Try it.

Adapted from www.globalideasbank.org

A Comprehension Check

Match the city with the random act of kindness that happened there.

_____ 1. San Francisco

_____ 2. Portland

_____ 3. Patterson

_____ 4. St. Louis

_____ 5. Seattle

_____ 6. Atlanta

a. a person pays for someone else's parking

b. a person cleans up some writing in a public place

c. one driver tells another not to be concerned about bumping into his car

d. a person gives a tollbooth worker money for several other people

e. people help some older people with some household tasks

f. a person sees garbage on the street and throws it away

B Vocabulary Study

Find the verbs in *italics* in the reading. Then match the verbs with the nouns on the right to make complete phrases.

_____ 1. *paid* (par. 1 & 9)

_____ 2. *copied . . . down* (par. 2 & 5)

_____ 3. *plants* (par. 8)

_____ 4. *clean up* (par. 8)

_____ 5. *carry out* (par. 9)

_____ 6. *comes to* (par. 9)

a. the words

b. flowers

c. an act

d. an intersection

e. a toll

f. trash

C Visualizing Information in a Text

> Visualizing means forming pictures in your mind. Sometimes visualizing detailed information in a text can help you understand it.

Look at the pictures. Under each one, write a phrase that describes an act of kindness from the reading.

1. _____

2. _____

3. _____

4. _____

5. _____

6. _____

D Relating Reading to Personal Experience

Discuss these questions with your classmates.

1. Which of the random acts of kindness described in the reading would you like to do someday? Which would you *not* like to do? Why not?

2. What random acts of kindness and beautification would help your school or community?

3. Have you ever done something to help a stranger? If so, what did you do?

Monkey Business

Predicting

Check (✓) the things you think a monkey can be trained to do. Compare your answers with a partner.

_____ 1. turn on the TV

_____ 2. turn the lights on and off

_____ 3. bring someone a sandwich

_____ 4. help a person get in and out of bed

_____ 5. bathe and dress a person

_____ 6. open a jar of juice

Skimming

Skim the reading to check your predictions. Then read the whole text.

1   When Sue Strong's Manhattan apartment grew very quiet one afternoon, she wasn't too surprised to find her monkey, Henrietta, in the bathroom surrounded by opened jars and licking lotion off her lips.

2   Life with Henrietta is never boring. But then again, Henrietta is not just any monkey. She is one of 50 working simians in the Helping Hands program, which trains monkeys to assist quadriplegics[1] with day-to-day tasks. "What Seeing-Eye dogs are to the blind,

_____

[1] *quadriplegic:* a person who is permanently unable to move his or her arms or legs

the monkeys are to people who can't use their hands or legs," said Jean Amaral, the program's administrator.

For the past 18 years, Henrietta, nicknamed Henri, has been living with Strong, who became paralyzed in a car accident. Henri can turn on the TV, switch the lights on and off, and bring Strong a drink when she's thirsty. "Henri is a great help to me," Strong said. "I can't imagine what life would be without her." Strong has a caretaker who comes to her home each morning and night to help her get in and out of bed and to bathe and dress her. When the assistant leaves, Henri takes over, allowing Strong to stay alone for hours. "Without an attendant or family member around to help, if I drop the stick I hold in my mouth to lift light switches, I would be alone and in the dark," she said. "With Henri, I can spend eight hours alone and be fine." 3

Henri spends most of her day playing or napping. When Strong needs something, she points at the object she wants with a mouth-operated laser light, which is attached to her chair. "Henri is trained to look for the laser light," Strong said. "When she sees the object I need, she knows what to do." Henri is trained to fetch and open jars of juice and place sandwiches in a holder. "With Henri, I usually find that I'm sharing my sandwich with her," Strong said. 4

The two have grown so close over the years that Strong considers Henri part of the family. Like all family members, Henri has her special habits "She eats more than anyone in the house," Strong said. "Italian, Mexican, Chinese, and pizza – anything but fish. And she never gains an ounce." 5

Not only does Henri help Strong with daily tasks, she also lifts Strong's spirits with her charm and playfulness. While people are sometimes shy about talking to Strong when she is out alone, everyone wants to talk to her when she is with Henri. 6

Henri loves to have her hair combed. She jumps into Strong's lap and waits eagerly for her turn when Strong is getting her hair brushed. She also likes to sit in warm piles of freshly dried clothes and watch other monkeys on TV, slapping the set happily when they're on the screen. "She's got a definite opinion on everyone who walks in the house," Strong said. "Some people she loves. Others she loves to nibble at their ankles. Henri even kicks some people she doesn't like!" 7

Adapted from *Daily News*

A Comprehension Check

Write the number of the paragraph where you can find the following information.

_____ a. how Strong communicates her needs to Henrietta

_____ b. what Henrietta likes to eat

_____ c. the kinds of problems Henrietta can cause for visitors

_____ d. the name of the program that trained Henrietta

_____ e. the length of time Henrietta has been with Strong

_____ f. a funny activity that Strong found Henrietta doing quietly

_____ g. how people react to Strong when she is out with Henrietta

B Vocabulary Study

Match the words and phrases from the reading that are similar in meaning.

_____ 1. *monkeys* (par. 2)   a. *assist* (par. 2)

_____ 2. *turn on* (par. 3)   b. *attendant* (par. 3)

_____ 3. *bring* (par. 3)   c. *day-to-day* (par. 2)

_____ 4. *caretaker* (par. 3)   d. *fetch* (par. 4)

_____ 5. *help* (par. 3)   e. *switch on* (par. 3)

_____ 6. *daily* (par. 6)   f. *simians* (par. 2)

C Summarizing

> When you summarize a text, you include only the most important information. A summary does not include details or examples. Summarizing is a strategy that can help you check your understanding of a text.

Use words from the reading to complete the summary.

Henrietta is a monkey that is trained to _____ Sue Strong with
                                                    1

everyday _____. Strong became _____ after an accident
                 2   3

and needs help at _____. Strong tells Henrietta what she wants by
                         4

using a _____. Strong and the monkey are very close. In fact, Strong
              5

considers Henrietta a member of the _____.
                                           6

D Relating Reading to Personal Experience

Discuss these questions with your classmates.

1. Do you think a person would be a better caregiver for Sue Strong than Henrietta? Why or why not?

2. Do you think it's a good idea to train animals to help people? Explain your answer.

3. Would you like to have a monkey help with tasks in your home? Why or why not?

> Reread one of the unit readings and time yourself. Note your reading speed in the chart on page 124.

3 Movies

Look at the titles of the readings and their brief descriptions to preview this unit's content. Before you begin each reading, answer the questions about it.

Reading 1

A Dangerous Career in the Movies

Do you seek danger and excitement? Are you a risk-taker? In this article, you can find out if being a stunt person in the movies is for you.

1. What kinds of things do stunt people do in movies?

2. What qualities does someone need to be a stunt person?

3. How do stunt people protect themselves?

Reading 2

Life as a Movie Extra

They have been in almost every movie you've seen, but you probably have not paid much attention to them. This newspaper article discusses the role of movie "extras."

1. Name a movie that you have seen recently that had a lot of extras.

2. What are some of the roles that extras can play on movie sets?

3. Why do you think people want to be movie extras?

Reading 3

The Storyteller

In this magazine article, find out what director Steven Spielberg enjoys most about filmmaking.

1. Have you seen any of these Spielberg movies: *E.T.*, *Raiders of the Lost Ark*, *Jurassic Park*? If so, what did you like, or dislike, about them? Have you seen any other Spielberg movies?

2. Which movie director(s) do you like?

3. Why do you think people become movie directors?

A Dangerous Career in the Movies

Predicting

Check (✓) the information you think is true about stunt people. Compare your answers with a partner.

_____ 1. Movie producers usually want actors to perform their own stunts.

_____ 2. Stunt people have to be willing to take risks.

_____ 3. Stunt people must be able to pay attention to detail.

_____ 4. A stunt person needs to be physically fit.

_____ 5. Stunt people almost never rehearse their stunts.

_____ 6. Stunts are always performed by live actors or stunt people.

Skimming

Skim the reading to check your predictions. Then read the whole text.

1   When you think about action movies, what comes to mind? Perhaps you think of scenes like this: Two people fighting on top of a moving train. Someone jumping out of a window or driving a car off the top of a multi-story parking garage. Action movies are exciting and a lot of fun to watch, but they also involve scenes of great risk and danger.

In the language of filmmaking, dangerous actions are called *stunts*. Who performs these stunts? This work is too dangerous for regular actors. Movie companies usually hire special stunt people to stand in for the actors in scenes that are unsafe.

Movie producers don't like to let actors do their own stunt work. If the actors injure themselves, it can delay the production schedule. Using stunt people also saves time. Most stunt people have years of experience, which enables them to perform their stunts with a minimum of risk. It would take too long to train the actors to perform dangerous scenes safely. 2

Some people who love the thrill of dangerous sports (such as sky diving or rock climbing) think it would be easy to work as a stunt person. But it isn't enough to be a risk-taker. Stunt work also requires careful planning, attention to detail, and extreme caution. In order to avoid accidents, every stunt is planned long in advance, and each scene is rehearsed many times. Stunt performers also have to know what to do if anything goes wrong. 3

In addition to risk-taking and meticulous attention to detail and planning, stunt work requires being in top physical condition. Although there are a few training programs for stunt performance, most offer only an overview of the profession. Normally, the people who attend these programs already have experience in dangerous sports, rescue work, or the military. So the best way to prepare for a career in stunt work is to train in an area that involves strong physical conditioning and has an element of physical danger. Martial arts, scuba diving, and wrestling are just a few examples. 4

Modern filmmaking techniques have changed the way some dangerous scenes are filmed. For example, computer-generated images (CGI) make it possible to show stunts that would be too dangerous or expensive for real stunt people to perform. CGI is often used today to create big fight scenes, car crashes, and explosions. 5

However, CGI is not always the best choice. Many film directors (and audiences) want to see real people perform actual stunts. In addition, the rising popularity of made-for-TV movies around the world ensures that there is still plenty of work for stunt people in the film industry today. 6

A Comprehension Check

Check (✓) the statement that best expresses the main idea of the reading.

_____ 1. Stunt people have to be physically fit so that they won't get hurt.

_____ 2. Movie producers prefer using stunt people to using actors.

_____ 3. Stunt work is dangerous and needs to be done by skilled people.

_____ 4. Movie companies sometimes use technology for stunts instead of stunt people.

B Vocabulary Study

Find the words and phrases in *italics* in the reading. Then circle the correct meanings.

1. If you *stand in* for someone, you **replace** / **stand near** / **work for** the person. (par. 1)

2. When you use *extreme caution*, you are very **careful** / **interested** / **slow**. (par. 3)

3. When something is planned *long in advance*, it was planned **over a long period of time** / **a long time before** / **to take a long time**. (par. 3)

4. If you give *meticulous* attention to something, you give it **very careful** / **expensive** / **little** attention. (par. 4)

5. An *overview* gives you **details** / **a general idea** / **a clear picture**. (par. 4)

6. When something is *generated*, it is **bought** / **made** / **seen**. (par. 5)

C Identifying Supporting Details

> Supporting details in a text explain the main ideas more fully. If you can identify supporting details, you will have a clearer understanding of the writer's main ideas.

Look back at the reading to find and underline two details that support each main idea below. Write the paragraph number for each supporting detail (SD). Compare your answers with a partner.

1. Producers want stunt people rather than actors to do stunts.

   SD 1: par. __1__   SD 2: par. _____

2. Stunt work requires these skills in addition to being able to take risks:

   SD 1: par. _____   SD 2: par. _____

3. These activities and professions are good ways to train for stunt work:

   SD 1: par. _____   SD 2: par. _____

4. Today, some stunts are made with computer-generated imaging.

   SD 1: par. _____   SD 2: par. _____

D Relating Reading to Personal Experience

Discuss these questions with your classmates.

1. Would you want to be a stunt person? Why or why not?

2. Have you seen a movie that had good stunts? If so, describe the stunts.

3. Do you prefer to see actual people perform stunts in movies or computer-generated images? Why?

Life as a Movie Extra

Thinking About What You Know

How much do you know about movie extras? Mark each statement *T* (true) or *F* (false). Compare your answers with a partner.

_____ 1. Movie extras get paid well.

_____ 2. Movie extras usually do not speak any lines.

_____ 3. Movie extras are sometimes main characters.

_____ 4. Being a movie extra can be boring.

_____ 5. Movie extras need acting experience.

_____ 6. Movie extras can work long hours.

Skimming

Skim the reading to check your answers. Then read the whole text.

Ordinary people have always been attracted to the world of movies and movie stars. 1
One way to get closer to this world is to become a movie extra. Although you have seen
movie extras, you may not have paid much attention to them. Extras are the people
seated at tables in a restaurant while the two main actors are in conversation. They are
the guests at the wedding of the main characters. They are the people crossing the street
while "the bad guy" is being chased by the police. Extras don't normally speak any lines,
but they help make the scenes look real.

Being a movie extra might seem like a lot of fun. You get to see what life is like behind 2
the scenes. But don't forget that being an extra is really a job, and it's mostly about doing
nothing. First-time extras are often shocked to learn how slow the process of movie
making is. In a finished movie, the action may move quickly. But it can sometimes take a
whole day to shoot a scene that appears for just a few minutes on the screen.

3　　　The main requirement for being an extra is the ability to wait. You may report to work at 5 or 6 a.m., and then you wait until the director is ready for your scene. This could take several hours. Then there may be technical problems, and you have to wait some more. After the director says "action" and you do the first "take," you may have to do it again if he or she is not satisfied with the scene. In fact, you may have to do the same scene over and over again. You could be on the set for hours, sometimes waiting outdoors in very hot or cold weather. You may not be finished until 11 p.m. or midnight. The pay isn't good, either – often only a little bit above minimum wage.[1] And you must pay the agent who gets you the job a commission of about 10 percent.

4　　　So who would want to be a movie extra? In spite of the long hours and low pay, many people still apply for the job. Some people truly enjoy the work. They like being on a movie set, and they enjoy the companionship of their fellow extras. Most of them have flexible schedules, which allow them to be available. They may be students, waiters, homemakers, retired people, or unemployed actors. Some unemployed actors hope the work will help them get real acting jobs, but it doesn't happen often. Most people in the movie industry make a sharp distinction between extras and actors, so extras are not usually considered for larger parts.

5　　　The next time you see a movie, don't just watch the stars. Take a closer look at the people in the background, and ask yourself: Who are they? Why are they there? What else do they do in life? Maybe there is someone in the crowd who is just like you.

_____

[1] *minimum wage:* according to U.S. law, the lowest hourly amount someone can be paid

A Comprehension Check

Two of the answers to each question are correct. Cross out the wrong answer.

1. What is true about movie extras?
   a. Sometimes agents get them jobs in movies.
   b. They often have to wait around on movie sets and do nothing.
   c. It's a good way to get a real acting job.

2. What might surprise movie extras the first time they do the job?
   a. It can take hours to do a scene that is only a few minutes long in the movie.
   b. They may have to do the same scene many times.
   c. The actors are interested in talking to them.

3. Why do most people work as movie extras?
   a. They like meeting other movie extras.
   b. They think they will become famous.
   c. They want to be on a movie set.

4. What are the job requirements for being a movie extra?
   a. You have to have a flexible schedule.
   b. You must be attractive.
   c. You must be willing to repeat a scene many times.

B Vocabulary Study

Find the words and phrases in the box in the reading. Then complete the sentences.

| attracted to (par. 1) | behind the scenes (par. 2) | shoot (par. 2) |
| fellow (par. 4) | parts (par. 4) | background (par. 5) |

1. She is a very popular star, and she is well liked by her _____ actors.

2. I didn't notice the people in the _____. I was paying attention to the two main characters that were arguing.

3. We need actors for six _____. They will play the people on the team.

4. It's interesting to see what happens _____ in the making of a movie. Many people that you never see are working very hard.

5. They were able to _____ the movie in just 10 days.

6. I wasn't _____ the movie business at first, but now I love it.

C Thinking Beyond the Text

▶ Good readers are able to go beyond the words that a writer actually uses and understand ideas that are never directly expressed. One way to practice this strategy is to imagine other information that the writer could have added about the topic.

Read the following sentences. They are not in the reading. If they were in the reading, in which paragraph would you expect to find each one?

_____ a. It's not a surprise that people don't do this job for very long.

_____ b. That person might even be a friend of yours.

_____ c. They are one of many people in a large crowd.

_____ d. It may take several days to shoot a very complicated scene.

_____ e. Sometimes even lawyers are extras just because they want to take a break from their everyday jobs.

D Relating Reading to Personal Experience

Discuss these questions with your classmates.

1. What do you think would be interesting about being a movie extra?

2. In which types of movies would it be fun to be an extra?

3. If you got a job as an extra, what part would you like to play?

The Storyteller

Predicting

Read the questions about Steven Spielberg. Then check (✓) the answers you think are correct. Compare your answers with a partner.

1. What was the inspiration for some of Spielberg's most successful movies?

   _____ a. ghost stories

   _____ b. childhood memories

   _____ c. fear of airplanes

2. How old was Steven Spielberg when he made his first movie?

   _____ a. 11

   _____ b. 15

   _____ c. 21

3. How much money did Spielberg earn the first time he worked in Hollywood?

   _____ a. a lot of money

   _____ b. very little money

   _____ c. no money

Skimming

Skim the reading to check your predictions. Then read the whole text.

1   Steven Spielberg has always had one goal: to tell as many interesting stories to as many people as possible. The son of a computer scientist and a pianist, Spielberg spent his early childhood in New Jersey and then Arizona. Some of his childhood memories became the inspiration for his filmmaking.

Even decades later, Spielberg says he has vivid memories of his earliest years, which 2
are the origins of some of his most successful films. He believes that *E.T.* is the result of
the difficult years leading up to his parent's 1966 divorce. He commented, "It is really
about a young boy who was in search of some stability in his life." *Close Encounters of the
Third Kind* was inspired by times when the four-year-old Steven and his father – a sci-fi
fanatic – would search the skies for meteors. His mother remembers, "He was scared of
just about everything. When trees brushed against the house, he would jump into my
bed. And that's just the kind of scary stuff he would put in films like *Poltergeist*." To this
day, Spielberg's wife, actress Kate Capshaw, says her husband remains terrified of airplane
and elevator rides and closed-in places.

Steven was 11 when he first got his hands on his dad's movie camera and began 3
shooting short flicks[1] about flying saucers and World War II battles. These homemade
movies gave him a way to escape his fears. From the very beginning, he had a creative
imagination. With his talent for scary storytelling, he could terrify his three younger
sisters. It also made it easier for him to make friendships. On Boy Scout camping trips,
when night fell, young Steven became the center of attention. "Stevie would start telling
his ghost stories," says Richard Y. Hoffman, Jr., leader of Troop 294, "and everyone would
suddenly get quiet so that they could all hear."

Spielberg moved to California with his father and went to high school there, but his 4
grades were so bad that he barely graduated. Both UCLA and USC film schools rejected
him, so he entered California State University at Long Beach because it was close to
Hollywood. Spielberg was determined to make movies, and he managed to get an unpaid,
non-credit internship in Hollywood. Soon he was given a contract, and he dropped out of
college. He never looked back.

Now, many years later, Spielberg is still telling stories with as much passion as when 5
he was a boy. Ask him where he gets his ideas, and Spielberg will shrug. "The process for
me is mostly intuitive," he says. "There are films that I feel that I need to make. And it's for
a variety of reasons, for personal reasons, or because I just want to have fun. Or maybe
because the subject matter is cool, and I think that my kids will like it. And sometimes I
just make movies because I think they will make a lot of money."

---

[1] *flicks:* a slang word for "movies"

Adapted from *Business Week*

A Comprehension Check

Write the number of the paragraph that answers each question.

_____ a. How did Spielberg use his stories to make friends?

_____ b. How does Spielberg get his ideas today?

_____ c. How did Spielberg get into the movie business?

_____ d. What has Spielberg always wanted to do?

_____ e. How did events in Spielberg's life inspire his movies?

B Vocabulary Study

Find the words in *italics* in the reading. Then match the words with their meanings.

_____ 1. *origins* (par. 2)

_____ 2. *stability* (par. 2)

_____ 3. *fanatic* (par. 2)

_____ 4. *terrify* (par. 3)

_____ 5. *shrug* (par. 5)

_____ 6. *intuitive* (par. 5)

a. raise the shoulders to express that you don't know something

b. the starting point for ideas

c. permanence; the state of not changing

d. frighten

e. able to know something without thinking very much about it

f. someone whose enthusiasm for something is extreme

C Making Inferences

> Sometimes the reader must infer, or figure out, what the writer did not explain or state directly in the text.

Check (✓) the statements you think Spielberg would say.

_____ 1. I've always been good at telling stories.

_____ 2. My parents weren't happy together. However, that didn't bother me at all.

_____ 3. If students don't do well in school, they won't succeed.

_____ 4. I have never understood why people get scared when they see my movies.

_____ 5. I wanted to work in the movies because I didn't finish college.

_____ 6. Making movies can be fun.

_____ 7. The most important thing in a movie is the story.

D Relating Reading to Personal Experience

Discuss these questions with your classmates.

1. Do you think that a movie has to have a good story? Give some examples to explain your answer.

2. Who is more important for a movie's success, the director or the actors? Why?

3. Would you like to work in the movie industry? Why or Why not? If you would, what kind of work would you like to do?

> Reread one of the unit readings and time yourself. Note your reading speed in the chart on page 124.

4 Families

Look at the titles of the readings and their brief descriptions to preview this unit's content. Before you begin each reading, answer the questions about it.

Reading 1

Living with Mother

This newspaper article reports on an unusual type of marriage custom in a region of southwest China.

1. How large is your family? Do you live with or near all of your relatives?

2. How close are you to your aunts and uncles?

3. In your culture, does property pass down through the mother or the father?

Reading 2

Father's Day

In this excerpt from a memoir, the writer describes the special relationship he had with the father figure in his life when he was growing up.

1. What are some things boys usually learn from their fathers?

2. Is there a special day to honor fathers in your culture? If so, what happens on that day?

3. What happens in your culture when there is no father in the house? Does another relative usually help bring up the children? Explain your answer.

Reading 3

The Sandwich Generation

Read this article about the "sandwich generation" that is being created by changes in society and family life.

1. How many generations usually live in the same household in your culture?

2. In your culture, what is the life expectancy of babies born today? Of people your age? Of your grandparents?

3. What problems do people often have when their parents become elderly?

Living with Mother

Thinking About What You Know

Do you know of cultures in which the following statements are true? Compare what you know with a partner.

1. After marriage, husbands do not live with their wives or children.

2. After marriage, wives live with their husband's family.

3. It is very easy to get a divorce.

4. The marriage ceremony is usually very expensive and lasts for many hours, sometimes days.

5. Children take their father's family name.

6. The head of the household is the oldest woman.

7. Children are brought up by their uncles.

Skimming

Skim the reading to find out which statements are true about the Mosuo people. Then read the whole text.

1. Tseta Dashi is twenty-nine and the proud father of a five-month old daughter. He does not see his baby much because both mother and daughter live in another village, about 12 miles away.

2. Dashi prefers to continue living with his mother, along with his mother's brother; his own two brothers; his younger sister, Pizuchuma; and her two daughters. And where is Dashi's father? He has always lived with his own mother and rarely visits these days. Dashi's older brother has two children, but the children live with their mother. The father of Pizuchuma's children still lives with his mother.

3. The Tseta's family life may seem complicated, but the way they live is normal in Luoshui village. This area of China is home to the Mosuo people. For the Mosuo, there is

no notion of formal marriage and no marriage ceremony. Instead, the Mosuo have what are called "walking marriages."

In Mosuo society, the adult children, men and women, live in their mother's home even after they have found a partner. Their walking marriages result in a lot of coming and going in the evenings. Most nights, Dashi's older brother walks across the village to visit his partner and children. He returns home for breakfast. Pizuchuma's partner, who also lives in the same village, arrives at the Tseta house in the evening and leaves in the morning. Dashi, with twelve miles to travel, has more of a "bicycle marriage" and only gets to see his partner and new baby about twice a month. 4

Walking marriages have many effects on family life. For example, Pizuchuma's youngest daughter is the same age as Dashi's. Dashi is clear about his feelings. "I am closer to my nieces than to my daughter because I must always consider their upbringing and their education." It is Dashi and his brothers who are financially responsible for Pizuchuma's children, not their father. And when Dashi was growing up, the most important man in his life was not his father, but his mother's brother. Similarly, Dashi's baby girl will be brought up by her uncles. 5

Children take their mother's family name, and property passes down through the mother. The head of the household is always the oldest woman – the *aju*. "In Mosuo society the uncle is more powerful than the father," says the Luoshui village headman. "Inside the home, the mother is more powerful than the uncle." 6

Walking marriages can start from the age of seventeen or eighteen. Couples decide how often they want to see each other. "Maybe not every day. But the relationships are stable," says Guambu Ager, a Mosuo scholar. When the first child is born, the father's family brings presents to the mother's family aju in a "declaration of the relationship." 7

Mosuo "divorce" is very simple. If couples stop getting along, they stop the walking marriages. It is easy to split up, explains Ager. "Men and women do not set up house together, so there is no question of property ownership or custody[1] of the children. There are no quarrels. It is very harmonious." 8

---

[1] **custody:** the right or responsibility to take care of someone

Adapted from *The Independent*

A Comprehension Check

Write the number of the paragraph where you can find the following information.

_____ a. the age at which walking marriages can begin

_____ b. the name of the place where Dashi lives

_____ c. a description of Dashi's living arrangements

_____ d. how walking marriages affect family life

_____ e. how walking marriages end

_____ f. an introduction to Tseta Dashi, his partner, and his daughter

_____ g. when fathers see their partners and children

_____ h. who has power in Mosuo society

B Vocabulary Study

Find the words in *italics* in the reading. Then match the words with their meanings.

_____ 1. *complicated* (par. 3)   a. difficult to understand because of having many parts

_____ 2. *notion* (par. 3)   b. the way a child is cared for and taught how to behave

_____ 3. *upbringing* (par. 5)   c. arguments

_____ 4. *split up* (par. 8)   d. belief or idea

_____ 5. *quarrels* (par. 8)   e. peaceful

_____ 6. *harmonious* (par. 8)   f. separate

C Visualizing Information in a Text

> ▶ Visualizing means forming pictures in your mind. Sometimes visualizing detailed information in a text can help you understand it better.

Write the numbers of the family members in the correct houses.

1. Tseta Dashi

2. Tseta Dashi's partner

3. Tseta Dashi's daughter

4. Tseta Dashi's mother

5. Tseta Dashi's father

6. Tseta Dashi's two brothers

7. Tseta Dashi's older brother's children

8. Tseta Dashi's older brother's partner

9. Pizuchuma, Tseta Dashi's sister

10. Pizuchuma's partner

11. Pizuchuma's two daughters

12. Tseta Dashi's father's mother

13. Tseta Dashi's mother's brother

14. Pizuchuma's partner's mother

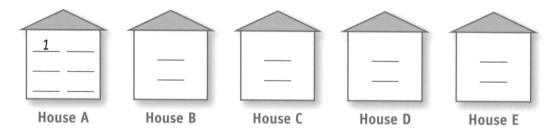

House A   House B   House C   House D   House E

D Relating Reading to Personal Experience

Discuss these questions with your classmates.

1. What are the advantages of Mosuo marriage customs? The disadvantages?

2. Do you think the Mosuo would like the marriage customs of your culture? Why or why not?

3. Do you think fathers or uncles can bring up children as well as mothers or mothers and fathers together? Why or why not?

Father's Day

Previewing Vocabulary

The words in the box are from the reading. Look up any new words in the dictionary. Then discuss the questions with your partner.

compassionate	determined	generous	open-minded
opinionated	softhearted	stubborn	

1. Which words in the box do you think describe positive qualities?

2. Which words in the box do you think describe negative qualities?

3. Are there words in the box that could be either positive or negative? Explain.

Scanning

Scan the reading to find and circle the words in the box. Which of the words describe the author? Which words describe his Aunt Marion? Which words describe both of them? Then read the whole text.

My father was 27 when he died. I was only a few months old. Over the years, the image I had of him was formed from all the stories I had heard. A single photograph of me in his arms is the only evidence I have that we ever met.   1

After my father's death, my mother moved back to Louisville, Kentucky, where she had grown up. We lived in a small house with her older sister, Marion, and their mother. This was a time when being a single parent was still considered unusual.   2

3   When I was small, there was a children's book called *The Happy Family*. Its image of the family was typical of the time. Dad worked all day long at the office, Mom baked in the kitchen, and brother and sister always had friends sleeping over. The family in the book looked nothing like my family, but luckily that wasn't the way I heard the story. The way my Aunt Marion read it to me, the story was very funny.

4   Compassionate and generous, opinionated yet open-minded, my aunt was the one who played baseball with me in the early summer evenings, who took me horseback riding, and who sat by my bed when I was ill. She helped me find my first job and arranged for her male friends at work to take me to the father-son dinners that marked the end of every sports season. When the time came, she convinced the elderly man next door to teach me how to shave. When I was 15, she gave me lessons on how to drive. Believing that anything unusual was probably good for me, she offered to get a loan so that I could go to Africa to work as a volunteer. She even paid for my first typewriter.

5   As a young girl, Aunt Marion always planned to have a large number of children of her own, but she never got married. This meant that she was free to spend her spare time taking care of me. Many people say we're very much alike: stubborn, determined, softhearted, and opinionated. We argued often. She always expected me to do my best. She never failed to assure me that I could do anything with my life that I wanted, if I only tried hard enough.

6   For more than sixty years, Aunt Marion was never without a job of some kind. In a fairer world, she would have been the boss. But being Aunt Marion, she didn't and still doesn't give herself much credit. Unless forced to stand in front in family photos, she's always in the background, and she doesn't think her efforts have made much difference. So every June for the past 40 years, with growing appreciation of my Aunt Marion, I've sent her a Father's Day card.

Adapted from *Paper Trail*

A Comprehension Check

Mark each statement *T* (true) or *F* (false). Then correct the false statements.

              father

__F__ 1. The writer's ~~mother~~ died when he was very young.

_____ 2. The writer lived in Louisville, Kentucky, before his father's death.

_____ 3. The writer grew up with his mother, aunt, and grandfather.

_____ 4. Aunt Marion did many of the things a father usually does.

_____ 5. Aunt Marion never wanted to get married and have children.

_____ 6. The writer and his aunt have similar personalities.

_____ 7. The writer and his aunt agreed about everything.

_____ 8. For many years, the author has sent his aunt a photo on Father's Day.

B Vocabulary Study

Find the words in *italics* in the reading. Then circle the correct meanings.

1. If you have friends *sleeping over*, they are sleeping **a lot** / **in your home** / **late**. (par. 3)

2. If you *convinced* someone to do something, you **did it for them** / **made the person decide to do it** / **taught them how to do it**. (par. 4)

3. When you are a *volunteer*, you **get paid** / **don't get paid** / **get paid a small amount** for work you do. (par. 4)

4. When people are *alike*, they **like each other** / **are nice** / **are similar**. (par. 5)

5. If I *assure* you that something will happen, I mean that **it will certainly happen** / **it may happen** / **it could happen**. (par. 5)

6. If you give *credit* to someone for doing something, you give the person **money** / **praise** / **understanding**. (par. 6)

C Making Inferences

> Sometimes the reader must infer, or figure out, what the writer did not explain or state directly in the text.

Check (✓) the statements that you can infer from the reading.

_____ 1. After his father's death, life was difficult for the writer's mother.

_____ 2. The writer had an unhappy childhood.

_____ 3. Aunt Marion didn't have any friends.

_____ 4. Aunt Marion didn't think she was a very important person.

_____ 5. Women were not bosses during the time that Aunt Marion worked.

_____ 6. For the writer, his Aunt Marion was like a father to him.

D Relating Reading to Personal Experience

Discuss these questions with your classmates.

1. Which person in your family do you feel closest to? What makes this person special?

2. Which person in your family are you most like? How are you similar?

3. What is a special memory you have from your childhood?

The Sandwich Generation

Thinking About the Topic

Check (✓) the statement that best describes what you think "The Sandwich Generation" means.

_____ 1. Today's generation of young adults doesn't cook, so they mainly eat sandwiches.

_____ 2. Elderly people are living longer nowadays, and young adults are living longer in their parents' homes.

_____ 3. Young adults feel sandwiched between their financial responsibilities and their desire to enjoy their life.

_____ 4. Middle-aged people have responsibilities for both their aging parents and their children.

Skimming

Skim the reading to find which statement is the best description of the sandwich generation. Then read the whole text.

1   Today people often look forward to their middle age as a time when they will be able to take things easier. After their children are grown, they expect to enjoy the life they have worked hard to create. However the reality is often very different. In middle age, many people discover that they have two ongoing responsibilities: one is to look after their aging parents, and the other is to help their young adult children deal with the pressures of life. Around the world, there are millions of people who are "sandwiched" in between the older and the younger generations. Sometimes there may be two or three generations living in the same household – a situation that is common in many Asian countries and in some parts of Europe. In other cases, a couple may be taking care of parents and children, but they do not live with them.

2   There are two important reasons for the rise of the sandwich generation. First, people are living longer than they used to. In the early nineteenth century, the average life

expectancy for adults in the United States, for example, was about 40, whereas today people live to an average age of 75. Therefore, children are taking care of their parents over a longer period of time. The second reason is that these days, young adults often live with their parents for a longer time than they did in the past. This is often for financial reasons. It's also more common for today's young adults to return home during or after college if they need financial or emotional support.

People who take care of elderly parents often face difficult issues. They may have to cover expenses that their parents cannot. They may have to manage their parents' financial and legal affairs. They may have to prepare for their parents' future needs, such as special medical care or a move to a nursing home. This can be a traumatic experience for everyone.

3

Caring for adult children presents challenges as well, and caregivers have to resolve important questions: How can financial responsibilities be shared among members of the household? How can household chores be shared? What is the best way to ensure everyone's privacy? Successfully coping with these issues can avoid a lot of stress for the whole family.

4

The financial and emotional pressures on the sandwich generation can be overwhelming. However, this time in life also has its rewards. It can be a time to rediscover the special qualities of one's parents or children. It can also provide a valuable opportunity to spend more time with them. However, in order to survive this difficult period in their lives, the members of the sandwich generation must remember that they also need to pay attention to their own needs and look after the quality of their own lives. They can't be totally selfless.

5

Adapted from extension.usu.edu/files/publications/publication/FR_Marriage_2006-01pr.pdf

A Comprehension Check

Circle the letter of the correct answer.

1. What are the two main reasons that there is a sandwich generation today?
   a. Young adult children usually need financial help, and elderly parents often have health problems.
   b. People are living longer than they used to, and children often live with their parents for a longer time than in the past.

2. How much longer does the average person in the United States live in the twenty-first century than in the nineteenth century?
   a. 40 years longer
   b. 35 years longer

3. What is often a very difficult emotional issue for people in the sandwich generation?
   a. deciding how to take care of the needs of their elderly parents
   b. deciding how to divide household tasks

4. What can people in the sandwich generation do to avoid stress?
   a. spend more time with their parents and children
   b. remember to take care of their own needs

B Vocabulary Study

Find the words and phrases in *italics* in the reading. Are the meanings of the words or phrases in each pair similar or different? Write *S* (similar) or *D* (different).

_____ 1. *look forward* (par. 1) / *expect* (par. 1)

_____ 2. *look after* (par. 1) / *take care of* (par. 3)

_____ 3. *whereas* (par. 2) / *however* (par. 5)

_____ 4. *a traumatic experience* (par. 3) / *a valuable opportunity* (par. 5)

_____ 5. *cover expenses* (par. 3) / *manage financial affairs* (par. 3)

_____ 6. *chores* (par. 4) / *rewards* (par. 5)

_____ 7. *pay attention to their own needs* (par. 5) / *be totally selfless* (par. 5)

C Identifying Supporting Details

> Supporting details in a text explain the main ideas more fully. If you can identify supporting details, you will have a clearer understanding of the writer's main ideas.

Look back at the reading to find and underline two details that support each main idea below. Write the paragraph number for each supporting detail (SD). Compare your answers with a partner.

1. In middle age, many people discover that they have two ongoing responsibilities.

   SD: par. __1__

   SD: par. _____

2. There are two important reasons for the rise of the sandwich generation.

   SD: par. _____

   SD: par. _____

3. People who take care of elderly parents often face difficult issues.

   SD: par. _____

   SD: par. _____

D Relating Reading to Personal Experience

Discuss these questions with your classmates.

> Reread one of the unit readings and time yourself. Note your reading speed in the chart on page 124.

1. Which information in the reading is also true about your culture? Which information is different?

2. What is the best way to ensure everyone's privacy in a family?

3. What are the advantages and disadvantages of adult children living with their parents?

5 Men and Women

Look at the titles of the readings and their brief descriptions to preview this unit's content. Before you begin each reading, answer the questions about it.

Reading 1 ▶ ## The Knight in Shining Armor

In this fairy tale from a popular book, the writer shares some ideas about the relationship between men and women.

1. What was your favorite fairy tale when you were a child?

2. Do you know any fairy tales about knights in shining armor? Do you know any fairy tales about princesses? What happens in these stories?

3. What are some things that typically happen to females in fairy tales? What typically happens to males?

Reading 2 ▶ ## Men, Women, and TV Sports

In this magazine article, the writer explains how men and women react differently to sports programs on TV.

1. Do you think men or women usually prefer watching sporting events on TV? Who usually prefers each of the following types of programs: action-adventure, suspense stories, drama, situation comedies, and soap operas?

2. Do you ever watch sports on TV? If so, what kinds of sports do you watch?

3. What do you like about watching sports on TV? What do you dislike about it?

Reading 3 ▶ ## Boys and Girls in Class

Are there gender differences in the way boys and girls learn? This article explores that question.

1. Do you think boys and girls behave differently in class? If so, explain some of the differences.

2. Do boys and girls like to study different subjects? Explain your answer.

3. Do you think it's important for teachers to give children a lot of encouragement at school? Why or why not?

The Knight in Shining Armor

Predicting

You are going to read a fairy tale about a knight, a princess, and some dragons. Look at the picture. Then answer the questions. Discuss the reasons for your answers with a partner.

1. What do you think happens to the princess?
   a. She is trapped by a dragon, but she kills it with a sword.
   b. She is trapped by a dragon and cries out for help.
   c. She stops loving the knight because he is afraid to kill dragons.

2. What do you think happens to the knight?
   a. He lets the dragon kill him because he doesn't feel worthy of the princess's love.
   b. He falls in love with the princess and marries her.
   c. He gets a lot of advice from the princess about how to kill a dragon.

3. What do you think happens to the dragon?
   a. It runs away and is never seen again.
   b. It is killed by the knight.
   c. It attacks the knight and the princess and kills them.

Skimming

Skim the reading to check your predictions. Then read the whole text.

1   A knight in shining armor was traveling through the countryside. Suddenly, he heard a woman crying out. He raced to the castle, where the princess was trapped by a dragon. The noble knight pulled out his sword and killed the dragon. As a result, he was received warmly by the princess.

2   As the gates opened, he was welcomed and celebrated by the family of the princess and the townspeople. He was acknowledged as a hero. He and the princess fell in love.

3   A month later, the noble knight went off on another trip. On his way back, he heard his beloved princess crying out for help. Another dragon was attacking the castle. When the knight arrived, he pulled out his sword to slay the dragon.

Before he swung, the princess cried out from the tower, "Don't use your sword, use this noose.[1] It will work better." 4

She threw him the noose and then motioned instructions on how to use it. He hesitantly followed her instructions. He wrapped it around the dragon's neck and then pulled hard. The dragon died, and everyone rejoiced. 5

At the celebration dinner, the knight felt he hadn't really done anything. Somehow, because he had used her noose and not his sword, he didn't feel worthy of the town's admiration. After the event, he was depressed and forgot to shine his armor. 6

A month later he went on another trip. As he left with his sword, the princess reminded him to be careful and to take the noose. On his way home, he saw yet another dragon attacking the castle. This time he rushed forward with his sword but hesitated, thinking that maybe he should use the noose. In confusion, he looked up and saw his princess waving from the castle window. 7

"Use the poison," she yelled. "The noose won't work." 8

She threw him the poison, which he poured into the dragon's mouth, and the dragon died. Everyone rejoiced and celebrated, but the knight felt ashamed. 9

A month later, he went on another trip. As he left with his sword, the princess reminded him to be careful, and to bring the noose and the poison. He was annoyed by her suggestions, but took them just in case. 10

This time on his journey, he heard another woman in distress. As he rushed to her call, his depression was lifted and he felt confident and alive. But as he drew his sword to slay the dragon, he hesitated again. He wondered whether he should use the sword, the noose, or the poison. What would the princess say? 11

For a moment he was confused. But then he remembered how he had felt before he knew the princess, when he carried only a sword. He threw away the noose and poison and charged the dragon with his sword. He killed the dragon, and the townspeople rejoiced. 12

The knight in shining armor never returned to his princess. He stayed in this new village and lived happily ever after. He eventually married, but only after making sure his new partner knew nothing about nooses and poisons. 13

_____

[1] **noose:** one end of a rope that is tied to form a circle that can be tightened around a neck to hang and kill

Adapted from _Men are from Mars, Women are from Venus_

A Comprehension Check

Put the events in order. Number the sentences from _1_ (first event) to _7_ (last event).

_____ a. The knight got married.

__1__ b. The knight killed a dragon with a sword.

_____ c. The knight killed a dragon with a sword again.

_____ d. The knight fell in love with the princess.

_____ e. The knight killed a dragon with a noose.

_____ f. The knight became depressed and forgot to shine his armor.

_____ g. The knight killed a dragon with poison.

B Vocabulary Study

Find the words and phrases in *italics* in the reading. Then circle the correct meanings.

1. When a hero is *acknowledged*, he is **approved and accepted** / **given a lot of money**. (par. 2)

2. If a man tries to *slay* something, he tries to **kill** / **save** it. (par. 3)

3. Someone who *is beloved* **loves** / **is loved by** one or more people. (par. 3)

4. She *motioned* to him by **staying very still** / **moving her hands or head**. (par. 5)

5. When the people *rejoiced*, they were very **afraid** / **happy**. (par. 5)

6. When she *yelled*, she said something **loudly** / **quietly**. (par. 8)

7. When you are *in distress*, you are **confused** / **in danger**. (par. 11)

C Making Inferences

> Sometimes the reader must infer, or figure out, what the writer did not explain or state directly in the text.

Discuss the answers to the questions with a partner.

1. Why do you think the princess tells the knight not to use his sword? (par. 4)

2. Why does the knight feel unworthy of the town's admiration? (par. 6)

3. Why does the knight's depression go away when he helps the woman in distress? (par. 11)

4. Why does the knight never return to the princess? (par. 13)

D Relating Reading to Personal Experience

Discuss these questions with your classmates.

1. What are some of the princess's personal qualities? For example, is she kind and thoughtful? What about the knight's personal qualities?

2. In this story, what is the writer saying about the relationship between men and women?

3. Do you know any women who act like the princess or men who act like the knight? If so, give examples and explain why these people are like the princess or the knight.

Men, Women, and TV Sports

Thinking About the Topic

Look at the title and the pictures. Then check (✓) the statements you think are true. Compare your answers with a partner.

_____ 1. Men watch sports programs on TV more than women do.

_____ 2. Men read the sports section of newspapers more than women do.

_____ 3. Men like to work on household chores while they watch a game on TV, but women do not.

_____ 4. During a game on TV, men eat and drink more than women do.

_____ 5. While they watch a game on TV, men yell out comments more than women do.

_____ 6. If their team loses, men get more upset than women do.

Skimming

Skim the reading to check your answers. Then read the whole text.

Sports is a major part of television programming. It is available on TV night and day, seven days a week. Tens of millions of people in the United States regularly watch the national broadcasts of major sporting events, but men outnumber women in the viewing audience. In addition to watching sporting events, men also watch action-adventure and suspense programs. Women, however, would rather watch dramas, situation comedies, and soap operas. Given these differences, it is not surprising that men and women will approach, experience, and respond to the same sports program in different ways. In telephone interviews with 707 adults, two professors of communication, Walter Gantz, Ph.D., and Lawrence Wenner, Ph.D., found that:

a Men expressed considerably more interest in television sports. Fifty-one percent of the men and 24 percent of the women said they were interested. Men were also more likely than women to suffer if sports were taken off television. Fifty-four percent of the men compared to 34 percent of the women said that they would miss it within a week.

b Men spend more time than women watching the sports segment of local newscasts. They also read the sports section of newspapers and talk about sports on a regular basis. Over 50 percent of the male viewers rated themselves "very knowledgeable" about sports. But only 18 percent of females thought they were "very knowledgeable."

c Men watch sports to relax, follow a favorite team, see athletic drama, get excited, let off steam, and have something to talk about.

d Women, on the other hand, are more likely to watch for companionship. They join friends and family who are already watching. Thus, it gives women something to do with their friends or family.

e While viewing a game, men typically talk about it, yell out in response to action, eat snacks and drinks, and put off household chores.

f Women usually work as they watch and limit their intake of junk food.

g Men are more likely to watch post-game news coverage or follow the action in the newspaper. A winning team puts men in a good mood and prompts them to want to celebrate the victory. But a losing team sometimes puts men in a bad mood, and they avoid their families for a while until they recover.

2   Walter Stipp, Ph.D., a director of research for a major television network, has an additional idea. He suggests that while men tend to focus more on the moment of victory and defeat, women show "a deeper interest in the athlete and the sport."

3   Still, there are many rabid female sports fans, and they act just as their male counterparts do. Professor Gantz suspects that in the end, it's the level of "sportsfanship," not gender, that determines TV-viewing behavior.

Adapted from *Journal of Broadcasting & Electronic Media* and *Psychology Today*

A Comprehension Check

What percentage of men and women expressed these ideas according to the Gantz and Wenner study? Fill in the chart with the correct percentages.

	Men	Women
1. We are very interested in TV sports.		
2. We are unhappy when there are no sports on TV.		
3. We know a lot about sports.		

B Vocabulary Study

Find the words in the reading that match these definitions. The number of blanks represents the number of words in the answer.

1. a part of something   _____ (par. 1-b)

2. get rid of energy, anger, or strong emotions   _____ _____ _____ (par. 1-c)

3. watching   _____ (par. 1-e)

4. the amount of food or drink consumed   _____ (par. 1-f)

5. causes   _____ (par. 1-g)

6. extremely enthusiastic   _____ (par. 3)

C Recognizing Contrast in a Text

> Sometimes writers contrast, or show the difference between, ideas in a text. They often use words or phrases, such as *but*, *however*, *on the other hand*, and *while*, to signal the contrast.

Read these excerpts from the reading. In each excerpt, circle the words and phrases that signal contrast. Then draw an arrow between the ideas being contrasted.

1. . . . [men also watch action-adventure and suspense programs.] [Women, (however,) would rather watch dramas, situation comedies, and soap operas.]

2. Men watch sports to relax, follow a favorite team, see athletic drama . . . and have something to talk about. Women, on the other hand, are more likely to watch for companionship.

3. A winning team puts men in a good mood and prompts them to want to celebrate the victory. But a losing team sometimes puts men in a bad mood, and they avoid their families for a while until they recover.

4. He suggests that while men tend to focus more on the moment of victory and defeat, women show "a deeper interest in the athlete and the sport."

D Relating Reading to Personal Experience

Discuss these questions with your classmates.

1. According to the reading, are you a typical male or female when it comes to sports? Explain your answer.

2. If the survey was done in another country that you are familiar with, what do you think the percentages would be for men and women?

3. Do you know any men or women who are rabid sports fans? What do these fans do that shows how excited they are?

Boys and Girls in Class

Predicting

Complete the statements with *boys* or *girls*. Compare your answers with a partner.

1. Most _____ want to study hard so that they can please their teachers.

2. _____ are usually less interested in studying unless the material they are studying is really interesting to them.

3. _____ often think that if they fail in something, they have disappointed their teachers and parents.

4. _____ are often unrealistic about their own academic abilities. They think they are better in school than they actually are.

5. _____ need more encouragement from teachers than _____ do.

Skimming

Skim the reading to check your answers. Then read the whole text.

1   Are there gender differences in the way boys and girls learn? This is a question that parents, teachers, and educational psychologists have asked themselves for many years.

2   For some time, people thought that some differences between boys and girls result from differences in the way they are raised. For example, parents often give young boys toy trucks to play with, while young girls get to play with dolls. But cross-cultural

studies have shown that giving toy trucks to girls and dolls to boys didn't change essential differences in their personalities. Many researchers agree that there are natural male-female differences, including differences in learning styles.

A high school choir director tells a significant story about learning style differences. With the girls, he'll begin teaching a new song by sharing a story about why the composer wrote the song or who it was written for. "Giving the girls some context, telling them a story about the piece, gets them interested. The boys are just the opposite," he said. "If you start talking like that with the boys, they'll start looking at their watches, [and] they'll start getting restless. Then one of them will say, 'Can we please just learn the song?'" **3**

Another difference in learning styles is the way boys and girls relate to teachers. Most girls want to study hard so that they can please their teachers. Girls are usually more interested than boys in trying to please adults. Pleasing adults is not a strong motivation for most boys, however. Boys are usually less interested in studying unless the material they are studying is really interesting to them. **4**

Girls and boys also react differently to unsuccessful learning experiences. Girls tend to think that if they fail in something, they have disappointed their teachers and parents. When boys fail a test or a class, however, they don't see their failure as having any wider implications. They failed the test; they failed the class. That's all it means for them. **5**

In studies of students' report-card grades, researchers found that girls generally do better than boys in all subjects and in all age groups. But interestingly, this does not make girls more self-confident than boys. Girls tend to have higher standards for themselves and to judge their performance more critically than boys do. And boys tend to have unrealistically high estimations of their own academic abilities and accomplishments. Girls need more encouragement from teachers than boys. Boys, on the other hand, often need a reality check. They need to understand that they are not always as brilliant as they think they are. **6**

The important point to take from this research is that there are no differences in what boys and girls can learn. But there are significant differences in the ways they learn and their attitudes toward learning. **7**

A Comprehension Check

Check (✓) the statement that best expresses the main idea of the reading.

_____ 1. Boys are better than girls in some subjects, and girls are better than boys in other subjects.

_____ 2. Boys and girls learn in different ways, and they do not have the same ideas about learning.

_____ 3. Girls get better grades in school because they have a better attitude toward learning.

_____ 4. Girls and boys are interested in learning different things.

B Vocabulary Study

Find the words and phrases in the box in the reading. Then complete the sentences.

essential (par. 2)	restless (par. 3)	motivation (par. 4)
wider implications (par. 5)	reality check (par. 6)	brilliant (par. 6)

1. Their poor test results were a/an _____ for the students. They realized that they have to start working harder.

2. Bad grades are only one result of not studying. There are _____ for the student's future success.

3. They are both _____ students. Everyone comments about their intelligence.

4. Her _____ for studying is to get good grades. That's the reason she works so hard.

5. They are _____ children. They always want to get up from their seats.

6. It's _____ to do well on the test. If you don't, you'll fail the class.

C Recognizing Purpose

> Writers create texts for different purposes. For example, sometimes a writer wants to give information. Other times, the writer wants to persuade the reader to do something. Recognizing a writer's purpose will help you better understand what you read.

Check (✓) the writer's main purpose in the reading. Discuss the reasons for your answer with a partner.

_____ 1. to give advice on how to teach boys and girls

_____ 2. to persuade teachers to teach boys and girls differently

_____ 3. to compare differences in learning styles between boys and girls

_____ 4. to teach boys and girls how to be successful learners

D Relating Reading to Personal Experience

Discuss these questions with your classmates.

1. Which information in the reading is true about boys and girls in your culture? Which information is not true?

2. Should teachers teach boys and girls in different ways? Why or why not?

3. What do students need to do in order to be successful learners? What do teachers need to do to help them?

> Reread one of the unit readings and time yourself. Note your reading speed in the chart on page 124.

UNIT 6 Communication

Look at the titles of the readings and their brief descriptions to preview this unit's content. Before you begin each reading, answer the questions about it.

Reading 1

Spotting Communication Problems

In this magazine article, you learn how to become a more effective communicator and avoid misunderstandings.

1. Do you think some people are better communicators than others? If so, what makes them more effective?

2. Where is poor communication the biggest problem – at home, school, or work? Why?

3. Would you rate your communication skills as good, average, or poor? Why?

Reading 2

Watch Your Language!

What language should parents who come from different countries speak at home? This newspaper article reports on one family's solution.

1. What are the advantages of knowing more than one language?

2. How common is it in your culture for people to be bilingual?

3. Do you think it is confusing for children to learn more than one language when they are young? Why or why not?

Reading 3

What Is Text Messaging Doing to Us?

This reading looks at the effects of text messaging on how we communicate.

1. What do you like about text messaging? What don't you like about it?

2. How fluent are you in Textspeak?

3. What special text messaging language in English do you know?

Spotting Communication Problems

Thinking About What You Know

How much do you know about communication? Match each poor habit with a resulting problem to make a complete sentence. Compare your answers with a partner.

_____ 1. Speaking too fast

_____ 2. Playing with pens while talking

_____ 3. Using unfamiliar words

_____ 4. Interrupting the other person

a. annoys other people.

b. confuses other people.

c. makes other people feel unimportant.

d. makes other people think what you are saying is unimportant.

Skimming

Skim the reading to check your answers. Then read the whole text.

1   Are you sometimes slow to communicate with others at work? You may be a _communications laggard_, a term used to describe professionals who perform well in most work areas, but lag behind in their communication skills. If that sounds like you, you're not alone. In fact, a report in the _Wall Street Journal_ noted that the single biggest reason people fail to advance in their careers is lack of good communication skills.

2   There are several signs you can use to determine whether you or others are blocking the communication process. Begin by asking yourself some questions about the way you communicate.

3   **Do you use ambiguous body language?** Remember, when you communicate, it's not just the words that convey a message; it's what media experts call "the composite you." This composite takes into account all elements of your body language. For example, if you stand with your back half-turned to someone, if you constantly look away, if your head is lowered, or if you look like you're about to walk away, your body language is sending a signal that you're not interested in having a conversation.

Do you maintain silent moments? The next time you have a conversation with a 4
co-worker, make a mental note of how many times you're silent. Periodic silences let
people ask questions, acknowledge that they understand what you're saying, and offer
ideas of their own.

Do you speak too fast? This is one of the most common communication barriers. 5
A slow rate of speech implies well-chosen words and strengthens the importance of
the message you're conveying. Talking to people in an unhurried manner also gives the
listener time to absorb what you have said.

Do you talk with toys? Do you play with pens, scratch your head, tap your fingers, 6
or clear your throat when you're talking with someone? These mannerisms may be
unconscious, but they can be quite annoying to others, who may take you less seriously.

Do you make eye contact? When you make eye contact, you're telling someone that 7
you're interested in him or her, that you think the person is important, and that you want
to hear what he or she has to say.

Do you avoid overspeak? Aristotle said, "Think as the wise do, but speak as the 8
common do." Don't use big or obscure words. If others look confused every time you
open your mouth, you may be guilty of using "overspeak," a communication barrier that's
sure to send people running to the nearest dictionary.

Do you interrupt? People who cut others off in mid-sentence not only send an unkind 9
message ("I really don't care about what you're saying"), they also cut themselves out of
the communication process. Remember that communication is an exchange, and we learn
more from listening than from talking.

Being a good communicator is a natural skill for only a few people. Most of us have to 10
work at it.

Adapted from Take Charge Assistant

A Comprehension Check

**Circle the number of the picture that shows good communication skills. For the other
pictures, write the part of the article that the man should read.**

Do you make eye contact? _____ _____

_____ _____

B Vocabulary Study

Find the words in the reading that match these definitions. The number of blanks represents the number of words in the answer.

1. develop more slowly than others   _____ _____ (par. 1)

2. something made of several parts   _____ (par. 3)

3. things that stop something from happening   _____ (par. 5)

4. understand and think about   _____ (par. 5)

5. behaviors   _____ (par. 6)

6. not known to many people   _____ (par. 8)

C Paraphrasing

> Paraphrasing means using your own words to say what you have read. This is one strategy you can use to improve your understanding of a text.

Circle the letter of the best paraphrase for each statement from the reading.

1. *If that sounds like you, you're not alone.* (par. 1)
   a. There are many people who are similar to you.
   b. If you talk a certain way, people will leave you alone.

2. . . . *the single biggest reason people fail to advance in their careers is lack of good communication skills.* (par. 1)
   a. If people are not successful at work, it is often because they don't have good communication skills.
   b. Everyone who advances in their careers has very good communication skills.

3. . . . *we learn more from listening than from talking.* (par. 9)
   a. Being a good listener can benefit you more than being a good speaker.
   b. People who learn to listen also learn to talk.

4. *Most of us have to work at it.* (par. 10)
   a. Most people must have good communication skills if they want a good job.
   b. Most people have to practice to have good communication skills.

D Relating Reading to Personal Experience

Discuss these questions with your classmates.

1. Have you ever had a misunderstanding with someone because of a communication problem? Give examples.

2. Which of your communication skills do you think you could improve?

3. What are some communication problems other than the ones mentioned in the reading?

Watch Your Language!

Predicting

Read the information about the writer of the article and his family. Then discuss the answers to the questions below with a partner.

The writer is English. His wife is Spanish. They live outside Barcelona with their two daughters. Barcelona is the capital of Catalonia, an autonomous region of Spain, where people speak Spanish and Catalan, but the native language of many people is Catalan.

1. What language do you think the writer speaks to his wife?

2. What language do you think the writer speaks to his children?

3. What language do you think the children use to speak to their father?

4. What language do you think the children use to speak to their mother?

Skimming

Skim the reading to check your predictions. Then read the whole text.

My situation is one that I could never have imagined: My two very young daughters 1
speak a language that I don't. I understand it perfectly, and could, if I had to, keep up a
broken version of it. But in our house, three languages exist together – English, Spanish,
and Catalan. We live in a small village outside Barcelona, where Catalan is the native
language of most villagers. I live with Sumpta, my wife, and our two daughters. Julia
is four and a half, and Rita is almost two. Julia talks a lot, and Rita is beginning to do
the same.

One morning I was shaving, and Julia was leaning in the bathroom doorway. "Daddy. 2
Mommy speaks English, but you don't speak Catalan," she said.

"Would you like me to speak Catalan?" I asked. 3

"No!" she said, horrified. "Some daddies speak Catalan, and some don't." Then she 4
turned and shouted downstairs. "Mama, avui vaig al cole?"[1] (Mommy, am I going to
school today?)

---

[1] Julia is speaking Catalan.

5   "No! Avui es dissabte!" came the reply. (No, today is Saturday.)

6   "Can I watch a DVD then?" I could tell by the language that it was me who got to decide this time.

7   "After breakfast."

8   "Aeeeee!" she said.

9   As we went downstairs, I thought back to how we had worried about our three languages before Julia was born.

10   First there was English. Sumpta and I met while speaking English, in England, and we lived in London before moving to Spain. When we moved here, English remained our private language.

11   Sumpta has always used both Catalan and Spanish. Like millions of Catalans, she grew up bilingual.

12   So when Sumpta was pregnant with Julia, we had plenty to think about. I had a fear that my girls would grow up without speaking English. This appeared as a real possibility. I had seen other families who had so assimilated themselves that they had forgotten to pass on their mother tongue until it was too late.

13   We relied heavily on English, our private language, hoping it would become one of Julia's languages. And because we believed that a language is learned before a child can speak, we talked a lot.

14   So far it has worked. Julia looks at me and speaks English, looks at her mother and speaks Catalan. When she meets a child she doesn't know in the playground, her first words are in Spanish. Rita understands all three, and uses a mixture of words and noises when she speaks. At the moment, Julia speaks to her more in English than Catalan, but it'll be revealing to see which language they choose to speak together as they get older.

15   I have reached the conclusion that adults get much more confused about languages than children. For Julia, the confusion is not that she speaks three languages, but that her father only uses two, and there are some people who restrict themselves to only one.

Adapted from *The Independent*

A Comprehension Check

Mark each statement *T* (true) or *F* (false). Then correct the false statements.

___F___ 1. In the writer's house, ~~two~~ *three* languages are spoken.

_____ 2. Sumpta speaks to her children and her husband in different languages.

_____ 3. The writer does not understand Catalan.

_____ 4. The writer does not speak Spanish.

_____ 5. Julia is upset because her parents don't speak to her in the same language.

_____ 6. If Julia asks a question in English, the writer knows she wants him to answer.

_____ 7. Julia is confused about which language to use with other children.

_____ 8. Julia thinks it's strange that some people speak only one language.

B Vocabulary Study

Find the words and phrases in the box in the reading. Then complete the sentences.

keep up (par. 1)	broken (par. 1)	assimilated (par. 12)
relied on (par. 13)	conclusion (par. 15)	restrict (par. 15)

1. People can't understand her because she speaks _____ Spanish.

2. I've tried to _____ the French I learned by watching French movies.

3. Maria moved to Canada three years ago, but she hasn't _____ yet. She doesn't speak English or have any Canadian friends.

4. After reading the job ads, my _____ is that it's helpful to be bilingual.

5. Our teachers _____ our use of our first language in class. We must use only English.

6. I couldn't speak Chinese, so I _____ my Chinese friends to explain the menu.

C Understanding Reference Words and Phrases

> Writers use different kinds of words and phrases to refer to information that is stated earlier in a text. Sometimes they use pronouns like *it*. Other times they use the definite article *the* before a noun. Understanding reference words is very important for reading comprehension.

What do these words refer to? Write the correct words or phrases.

1. *it* (par. 1, line 2) — _the language that the writer's daughters speak_

2. *do the same* (par. 1, lines 6–7) — _____

3. *we* (par. 12, line 1) — _____

4. *This* (par. 12, line 2) — _____

5. *all three* (par. 14, line 3) — _____

D Relating Reading to Personal Experience

Discuss these questions with your classmates.

1. Do you agree that adults get much more confused about languages than children? Why or why not?

2. Whom do you know who speaks more than one language? At what age did the person learn the languages?

3. If you could have learned another language as a child, which language would you have chosen? Why?

What Is Text Messaging Doing to Us?

Thinking About the Topic

Check (✓) the statements you think are true about text messaging. Compare your answers with a partner.

_____ 1. Text messaging is the most common form of communication for teens.

_____ 2. Frequent texters find that it is hard for them to switch back to the real world of correct grammar, spelling, and writing skills.

_____ 3. Text-messaging all started with e-mail, online chat rooms, and online games.

_____ 4. "How RU" means "How are you?"

_____ 5. Everyone is becoming fluent in Textspeak.

_____ 6. Text messaging can be a positive sign of people's creativity and self-expression.

Skimming

Skim the reading to check your answers. Then read the whole text.

1   Do you sometimes get text messages like this: "M2AF – ttyawfn"[1]? Can you understand them? For today's teens and for many adults, too, text messaging is their most common form of communication.

---

[1] *M2AF – ttyawfn:* Message to all friends: Talk to you a while from now.

Although text messaging is convenient and fun, not everyone is in favor of it. To be a successful texter, you need to know the current lingo² that people are using and how to abbreviate words. But some teachers feel that text messaging is preventing young people from learning to write correctly. And some employers complain that employees are now using text message lingo at work. Frequent texters find that it is hard for them to switch back to the real world of correct grammar, spelling, and writing skills. How did things come to be this way?   2

It all started with e-mail, online chat rooms, and online games. People began to cut back on unnecessary words and phrases. For example, "How RU" soon replaced "How are you?" and "2nite" replaced "tonight." Shortened forms of words became the norm. Texting continued to grow in popularity, and people invented more and more words. Today it is like a real language with its own grammar and vocabulary. The growth of texting has raised an important question: As more and more students become fluent in Textspeak, do their writing skills suffer?   3

Educators disagree about the influence of Textspeak on students' writing skills. Some feel that students are losing the capacity to express themselves in complex, grammatically correct sentences. Others say there is little evidence that texting is having a negative effect on the language children use in their schoolwork. Some see it as a positive sign of people's creativity and self-expression. They believe students can keep the two systems separate – one for texting and one for school – and that it is helping students to appreciate writing more. It gets them to read and write more than they did before they had cell phones and computers.   4

Some educators suggest that the best way to deal with the issue is to promote technology, both inside and outside of the classroom, and to find ways of using it as a positive learning tool. For example, children can be allowed to type their assignments in an e-mail or cell-phone message and send them to their teacher. But they must use correct spelling and standard forms of words when they do so. In this way, students are using the technology they are familiar with but communicating in a form of language appropriate for schoolwork. These educators want to send a clear message: Textspeak is fine for social communication, but correct grammar and spelling are essential for communication in school.   5

_____

² *lingo:* slang, informal language

A Comprehension Check

Write the number of the paragraph where you can find the following information.

_____ **a.** how the language of text messaging started

_____ **b.** how to use text messaging to promote written communication

_____ **c.** the different opinions about the effects of text messaging on communication

_____ **d.** which groups are the most frequent users of text messaging

_____ **e.** what people do not like about text messaging

B Vocabulary Study

Find the words and phrases in *italics* in the reading. Then match the words and phrases with their meanings.

_____ 1. *is in favor of* (par. 2)   a. reduce

_____ 2. *abbreviate* (par. 2)   b. get worse

_____ 3. *come to be* (par. 2)   c. brought to someone's attention

_____ 4. *cut back on* (par. 3)   d. make a word shorter

_____ 5. *raised* (par. 3)   e. ability

_____ 6. *suffer* (par. 3)   f. begin to happen

_____ 7. *capacity* (par. 4)   g. supports

C Recognizing Purpose

> Writers create texts for different purposes. For example, sometimes a writer wants to give information. Other times, the writer wants to persuade the reader to do something. Recognizing a writer's purpose will help you better understand what you read.

Check (✓) the writer's main purpose in the reading. Discuss the reasons for your answer with a partner.

_____ 1. to persuade people that text messaging is a problem

_____ 2. to persuade people that text messaging is not a problem

_____ 3. to present different points of view about text messaging

_____ 4. to persuade schools to promote the use technology in the classroom

D Relating Reading to Personal Experience

Discuss these questions with your classmates.

1. Has text messaging made you a better or worse communicator? Give examples.

2. Should text messaging be allowed in schools? Why or why not?

3. Would it be a problem if Textspeak became the only form of written communication? Why or why not?

> Reread one of the unit readings and time yourself. Note your reading speed in the chart on page 124.

Dishonesty

Look at the titles of the readings and their brief descriptions to preview this unit's content. Before you begin each reading, answer the questions about it.

Reading 1

The Telltale Signs of Lying

Do you usually know when someone is lying to you? This magazine article describes clues that can help you decide if someone is telling the truth or a lie.

1. Do you know anyone who often tells lies? If so, who is it?

2. Why do you think people lie?

3. Have you ever thought that someone was telling a lie? If so, what were the clues in the person's behavior that made you think so?

Reading 2

Too Good to Be True

When companies advertise their products, they may say misleading things that may not be entirely true. This newspaper article investigates the facts behind some advertisements.

1. Name an advertisement that you like. Why do you like it? What claims, or statements, does the ad make about its product?

2. Do you usually believe what advertisements say? Why or why not?

3. What would you do if you found that a claim in an ad wasn't true?

Reading 3

Truth or Consequences

Are students cheating more these days than in the past? The writer of this newspaper article discusses cheating in schools today.

1. Why do you think some students cheat?

2. What are the consequences, or effects, of cheating in your culture?

3. Do you know anyone who has ever been caught cheating? What happened?

The Telltale Signs of Lying

Predicting

Answer these questions with a partner.

1. Look at the title of the reading. Think about the meaning of the verb *tell* and the noun *tale*? What do you think *telltale signs* means?

2. Look at the subheadings in the reading. *Nonverbal* means "without spoken words." When someone is lying, what nonverbal clues might you see?

3. Look at the woman in the picture. What are some nonverbal clues that show she might be lying?

4. After looking at the title, the subheadings, and the picture, what do you think the main idea of the reading will be?

Skimming

Skim the reading to check your prediction of the main idea.

1   Psychologists tell us that lying is a typical human behavior and happens for two reasons: to receive a reward or to avoid punishment. Whether we lie depends on whether we think it will be an advantage or a disadvantage to us.

2   Lying creates stress because most of us are taught to believe that it's wrong. When people are lying, and therefore, under stress, they normally give several verbal and nonverbal clues. For example, consider the case of Delbert, an employee of a large company. The director of the company started receiving threatening letters from one of the workers. An investigation led to one department with about a dozen workers. Delbert was interviewed first.

Verbal Clues

3   During the interview, Delbert gave some typical verbal clues that he was lying. Here are some examples:

Q: Do you know why anyone would write the director a threatening note?

A: Do I know why anyone would write the director a threatening note?

In the example above, Delbert repeated the question. Liars frequently do this because it gives them time to think of a false answer.

Q: Do you remember where you were on the date this last letter was mailed?

A: I might have been working, or I might have been off. I just don't remember.

In the second example, Delbert didn't answer the question directly. If he had mailed the letter, he would certainly remember where he was at the time. But he gave a vague answer to avoid being caught in a lie. Vague answers like this are also typical of liars.

Nonverbal Clues

When people are under stress because they feel threatened, they often react with a "fight or flight" mentality. It's difficult for them to stay still. For example, when people are asked difficult questions, they may look as if they want to leave the room. This happened with Delbert. While his head was facing the interviewer, his feet were pointed in the direction of the door as if he were ready to rush out.   4

Delbert tried to relieve stress through movement in another way, as well. When he was listening, he hardly moved at all. But when he was asked a difficult question, he shifted his position in the chair, moving his whole body.   5

A similar reaction to stress involves crossing the arms. When people feel threatened, they often subconsciously use their arms for protection. In response to some questions, Delbert crossed his arms as if to protect himself from attack.   6

It may seem childish, but some liars cover their mouths when telling a lie. That's because in times of stress, many people behave like children. Delbert frequently covered his mouth with his hand like a child, as if to keep his lie from coming out.   7

By thinking about Delbert's behavior during the interview, we can learn a valuable lesson. If you observe and listen carefully, you can improve your ability to recognize lies.   8

Adapted from *Journal of Accountancy*

A Comprehension Check

Circle the letter of the phrase that best completes each statement.

1. One reason that people lie is _____.
   a. to relieve stress
   b. to benefit from a situation
   c. to improve their lives

2. Delbert seemed to be lying because _____.
   a. his handwriting matched the writing in the letters
   b. he often didn't answer the interviewer's question
   c. his physical and verbal behavior was typical of liars

3. Two common behaviors of liars are _____.
   a. crossing the arms and giving answers that aren't clear
   b. listening to and carefully watching the person they are talking with
   c. sitting without moving and talking slowly

B Vocabulary Study

Find the words in *italics* in the reading. Then circle the letters of the correct meanings.

1. *punishment* (par. 1)
   a. what you get for doing something bad
   b. what you get for doing something good

2. *threatening* (par. 2 & 3)
   a. promising that something unpleasant will happen
   b. promising that something good will happen

3. *been off* (par. 3)
   a. taking a nap
   b. not working

4. *vague* (par. 3)
   a. interesting
   b. not clear

5. *mentality* (par. 4)
   a. a way of listening
   b. a way of thinking

6. *subconsciously* (par. 6)
   a. without being aware
   b. showing interest

C Identifying Supporting Details

One way writers support their general statements is by giving examples. If you can identify the examples in a text, you will have a clearer understanding of the writer's ideas.

Look back at the reading and find examples to support these general statements from the reading.

1. *When people are lying . . . they normally give several verbal and nonverbal clues.* (par. 2)

   a verbal clue: _____

   a verbal clue: _____

   a nonverbal clue: _____

   a nonverbal clue: _____

2. *. . . in times of stress, many people behave like children.* (par. 7)

   behavior: _____

D Relating Reading to Personal Experience

Discuss these questions with your classmates.

1. If you thought someone was lying to you, what would you do?

2. Are there situations when it is OK to tell a lie? If so, what are they?

3. Can you think of other clues that tell when a person is lying? If so, what are they?

Too Good to Be True

Thinking About the Topic

Discuss these questions with a partner.

1. What sorts of advertising claims do you think a company that makes **paper towels** might make about its product?

2. What sorts of claims do **makeup** companies make about their products?

3. What sorts of claims do companies that make **pain medications** make?

4. What do you think is the purpose of **the national advertising division of the Council of Better Business Bureau**?

Scanning

Scan the reading to find and circle the words in bold in the questions above. Check your answers to the questions. Then read the whole text.

Does one brand of paper towels really absorb more water than any others you can buy? Do physicians truly prefer one cold medicine to all the others? Will one kind of makeup really not rub off on your clothes? Well, that's what the ads say. 1

Advertisements make all sorts of claims, but nowadays a company can't just say that its product is the best. It often has to prove its claim. Many people don't realize that advertising claims are challenged all the time. 2

In the United States, one of the organizations that judges such challenges is the national advertising division of the Council of Better Business Bureau. This organization was created in 1971 by advertisers as a way to regulate themselves. For decades, the organization's advertising experts have examined what companies say about their 3 products. They try to answer questions, such as "Is it true that ColorStay makeup 'won't rub off on your collar'"?

4   Another makeup company wanted to test the ColorStay claim. It asked hundreds of women to put on ColorStay makeup and white shirts. Then they had to spend the day doing their usual activities. Based on this test, the competitor claimed that ColorStay makeup actually does rub off. ColorStay's manufacturer conducted a similar test on hundreds of women. The results of this test were the opposite: the makeup stayed on during normal use.

5   The different results of the tests puzzled the members of the Council of Better Business Bureau's advertising division. They wondered how people would understand the word "rub off" when they saw the ad. The Council finally decided that ColorStay's manufacturer had proved the makeup didn't rub off during "normal use." Because of this decision, the company added the words "under normal conditions" to its advertisements.

6   Over time, the Council has handled many other cases of "true" advertising claims that gave a false impression. For example, it once reviewed a TV commercial for a new brand of pain medication, Orudis KT. The ad claimed, "There are many prescription pain medications, and a doctor can prescribe any of them. Yet, 82 percent of doctors surveyed have prescribed Orudis."

7   The statement about Orudis KT was true. However, the ad didn't report that the doctors may have prescribed Orudis to patients one time only, but never again. The Council decided that the statement was misleading because it gave the wrong impression: It suggested that doctors preferred Orudis to all other pain medications. And this was not true. As a result, the company stopped using these ads, which really did sound too good to be true.

Adapted from *Minneapolis Star Tribune*

A Comprehension Check

Mark each statement *T* (true) or *F* (false). Then correct the false statements.

__F__ 1. Companies don't often have to prove their advertising claims.

_____ 2. The ColorStay ad claimed that women wouldn't get the makeup on their clothes.

_____ 3. The manufacturer of ColorStay did tests that found its ad was true.

_____ 4. Another makeup company did tests that found the ColorStay ad was untrue.

_____ 5. The advertising division of the Council of Better Business Bureau decided that the ColorStay ad was completely false.

_____ 6. After the advertising division gave its opinion of the ad, the manufacturer of ColorStay changed its ad.

_____ 7. Eighty-two percent of doctors prescribed Orudis pain medication at least once.

_____ 8. Eighty-two percent of doctors preferred Orudis to other pain medications.

B Vocabulary Study

Find the words in the reading that match these definitions.

1. questioned _____ (par. 2)

2. make rules for _____ (par. 3)

3. organized and directed _____ (par. 4)

4. usual _____ (par. 4)

5. idea _____ (par. 6)

6. asked questions _____ (par. 6)

C Understanding Pronoun Reference

> Writers use different kinds of pronouns to refer to information that is stated earlier in a text. Some common pronouns are *it, they,* and *their.* Understanding pronoun reference is very important for reading comprehension.

What do these pronouns refer to? Write the correct word or phrase.

1. *It* (par. 2, line 2) _____

2. *their* (par. 3, line 4) _____

3. *They* (par. 3, line 5) _____

4. *It* (par. 4, line 1) _____

5. *it* (par. 6, line 2) _____

6. *this* (par. 7, line 4) _____

D Relating Reading to Personal Experience

Discuss these questions with your classmates.

1. Have you ever seen a misleading advertisement? If so, why was it misleading?

2. Do you think it is important to regulate advertisers? Why or why not?

3. Do you consider an advertiser's claims when choosing a product? What else do you consider?

Truth or Consequences

Thinking About What You Know

How much do you know about cheating? Work with a partner. Circle the information that you think is correct.

1. Cheating in schools is **more** / **less** common today than in the past.

2. Cheating happens in **a few** / **many** schools.

3. **More than** / **less than** 50 percent of high school students have cheated at least once.

4. People **agree** / **disagree** about the reasons for cheating.

5. When students cheat, there are **few** / **many** serious consequences.

Skimming

Skim the reading to check your answers. Then read the whole text.

1   What's the most creative technique for cheating that you know? At one American high school, Ivan Baumwell watched a friend print out the answers to a history test in tiny type and tape them inside her water bottle. Devon Watts opened her watch before an exam and put a cheat sheet in front of the watch face. Lindsey Kleidman's classmates pretended they needed a tissue during a test. They took tissues from their teacher's desk, so that they could read the answer key on the desk, upside down. But one method was even more original. In Trevor Snell's class, students were allowed to bring food into the exam. He watched another student take advantage of this rule by hollowing out an apple and stuffing the answers to a physics test inside.

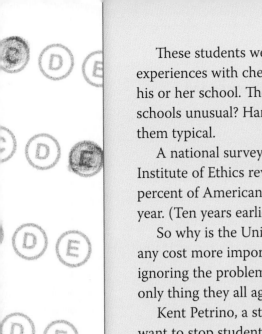

These students were among the dozens across the country who talked about their experiences with cheating. Everyone interviewed said that cheating was widespread in his or her school. The majority admitted cheating at some point themselves. Are these schools unusual? Hardly, according to a disturbing new report on cheating. It just makes them typical.

2

A national survey of 8,600 students released by Michael Josephson of the Josephson Institute of Ethics reveals how common cheating has become at high school. Seventy-one percent of American teenagers admitted cheating on at least one exam within the last year. (Ten years earlier the figure was 60 percent.)

3

So why is the United States becoming a nation of cheaters? Is pressure to succeed at any cost more important than pride in one's accomplishments? Are too many teachers ignoring the problem? Every student we spoke with has his or her own explanation. The only thing they all agreed on was that cheating is everywhere.

4

Kent Petrino, a student, blames teachers. "They need to pay more attention if they want to stop students from cheating," he says. "A lot of kids cheat because they know they won't get caught doing it."

5

It's not surprising that teachers reject this excuse. "It's true some teachers don't pay enough attention to cheating," says Kent's teacher, Judy Carrico. "But our job is to teach and not to be police officers. I really think parents have to teach this to their kids. And kids need to monitor themselves. We have so much to do that we can't do it for them."

6

Students know that if they cheat, they risk punishment. If they are caught, the school may tell their parents. They may also prohibit the students from attending school for a period of time or give an automatic failing grade. Are there any additional long-term consequences? "Of course there are," says Laura Mills. "Cheaters are just cheating themselves out of skills they need. I had to pass tests for my lifeguard training. If I'd cheated on my test, I wouldn't be prepared to deal with life-and-death decisions."

7

Josephson agrees. "Do we really want the next generation of doctors and airplane pilots and nuclear-missile designers to be people who cheated their way through school?" he asks.

8

Adapted from *The New York Times Upfront*

A Comprehension Check

Write the number of the paragraph where you can find the following information.

_____ a. conclusions about cheating based on interviews with students

_____ b. an argument that teachers are responsible for the problem

_____ c. an argument that teachers are not responsible for the problem

_____ d. possible reasons why students cheat

_____ e. consequences of cheating for the world

_____ f. consequences of cheating for students

_____ g. examples of types of cheating

_____ h. percentages that show how common cheating is in high school

B Vocabulary Study

Find the words and phrases in *italics* in the reading. Then match the words and phrases with their meanings.

____ 1. *upside down* (par. 1)		a. certainly not
____ 2. *hollowing out* (par. 1)		b. it doesn't matter what happens
____ 3. *widespread* (par. 2)		c. watch and check
____ 4. *hardly* (par. 2)		d. making an empty space inside something
____ 5. *at any cost* (par. 4)		e. with the part that's usually at the top at the bottom
____ 6. *monitor* (par. 6)		f. very common

C Visualizing Information in a Text

> Visualizing means forming pictures in your mind. Sometimes visualizing detailed information in a text can help you understand it better.

Number the pictures of cheating techniques in the order they are mentioned in the reading, from *1* (first) to *4* (last).

____ a.

____ b.

____ c.

____ d.

D Relating Reading to Personal Experience

Discuss these questions with your classmates.

1. What other cheating techniques have you heard of?

2. What do you think should be done to reduce cheating?

3. What would you do if a student who cheated on a test got a higher score than you?

> Reread one of the unit readings and time yourself. Note your reading speed in the chart on page 124.

UNIT 8 Etiquette

Look at the titles of the readings and their brief descriptions to preview this unit's content. Before you begin each reading, answer the questions about it.

Reading 1

Cell Phone Yakkers Need Manners

More and more people have cell phones today. This newspaper article explores a growing problem with cell phone use around the world.

1. Do you have a cell phone? If so, when and where do you use it?

2. Do cell phone users sometimes annoy you? Give examples.

3. What do you usually do when you are in a public place and someone with a cell phone disturbs you?

Reading 2

How Table Manners Became Polite

What is rude behavior at the dinner table and what is polite? How has the concept of table manners changed over the years? This newspaper article discusses these questions.

1. What rules are young children in your culture taught to follow when they are eating?

2. Does your family have any special rules for manners at mealtimes? If so, what are they?

3. How are table manners different in different cultures? Give some examples.

Reading 3

Dinner with My Parents

Inviting a boyfriend or girlfriend to have a meal with your parents is always a risk. This excerpt from Amy Tan's novel *The Joy Luck Club* describes one such meal.

1. Do you like to have guests for dinner? Why or why not?

2. In your culture, do dinner guests usually help themselves to food on the table? Explain your answer.

3. What do you do when your host offers you seconds or thirds? Do you accept the food to be polite? Or do you refuse it?

Cell Phone Yakkers Need Manners

Thinking About the Topic

**Look at the title and the picture. Then check (✓)
the statements you agree with. Compare your answers with a partner.**

_____ 1. Cell phone users should never talk in public places.

_____ 2. Most people have gotten used to loud cell phone users. They don't mind.

_____ 3. Cell phone users should not allow others to overhear their conversations.

_____ 4. People speak more loudly on cell phones than in ordinary conversation.

_____ 5. It's OK to use a cell phone in a public place if you speak softly.

Skimming

**Skim the reading to find out which statements the writer agrees with. Then read the
whole text.**

1   "Hi, it's Deirdre." With a cell phone held to her ear, Deirdre announced herself to everyone
she called. She was in a crowded airport, talking loudly about her day-care troubles, her family,
and her mother's surgery.

2   For the people sitting near her, there was no way to ignore this modern-day horror: the
public cell phone yakker who talks loudly about private matters in front of people who are
forced to listen.

3   When someone nearby finally asked her to have her next private conversation somewhere
else, it was Deirdre who was offended. "That's the rudest thing I've ever heard," she said.

4   People like Deirdre continue to have loud cell phone conversations in public. In fact,
the question of rudeness has led to a lot of discussion about cell phone etiquette. Many
people feel very strongly about the problems. Etiquette experts have written about the
issues, too. For example, Mary Mitchell, author of five books on etiquette, said, "We are
overhearing conversations we should not be overhearing, even though we don't want to be
overhearing them."

It is very hard to avoid listening to cell phone users, who tend to speak louder than they would to someone face-to-face. So people are overhearing lots of one-sided conversations on marital breakups, business deals, and what's for dinner. 5

There are billions of cell phone users in the world today, and people use their phones everywhere! Museums, movie theaters, schools, restaurants, and parks are struggling to limit annoying uses of cell phones. But the only real solution to the problem is this: cell phone users need to learn better manners. 6

Here are some basic rules for cell phone etiquette: 7

- Use your cell phone in public only when necessary.
- If you are not expecting an urgent call, turn off the phone during business meetings, at social gatherings, in restaurants, and at the theater. In these situations, set your phone to vibrate mode.
- If you absolutely must keep your phone on during a meeting, explain in advance.
- If you must make a call at a social gathering or at a restaurant, excuse yourself and find a reasonably private space in which to make the call.
- If you must speak while others are near, speak softly. Your conversation may be fascinating to you, but it is of no interest to others.
- If you use your cell phone while driving, you deserve whatever happens. Others do not. Pull over and take the few minutes you need to make your call.

Remember telephone booths? They were created with the idea that only the person you were calling should hear what you were saying. That's still a useful concept to keep in mind when using your cell phone. 8

Adapted from *The Philadelphia Inquirer*

A Comprehension Check

Choose the best advice from the box for each situation according to the reading.

> a. Find a private place to make your call.
> b. Set your cell phone to vibrate mode.
> c. Speak softly.
> d. Explain in advance why you have to leave your cell phone on.
> e. Find a safe place to stop. Then return the call.

_____ 1. You have an important meeting at work. You're expecting an important call from a sick family member, so you want to leave your cell phone on.

_____ 2. You're waiting for some friends in a restaurant. You want to call them and ask where they are.

_____ 3. You're driving, and your cell phone rings.

_____ 4. You're a doctor, and you're going to the theater. The hospital staff uses your cell phone number for emergency calls.

_____ 5. You're on the bus with a friend, and she just told you some wonderful news. You want to call another friend to share the good news.

B Vocabulary Study

Find the words and phrases in *italics* in the reading. Then circle the correct meanings.

1. If something is a *horror*, it causes people a lot of **illness** / **sadness** / **trouble**. (par. 2)

2. If people are *offended*, they feel someone has been **angry with** / **rude to** / **friendly to** them. (par. 3)

3. If people are *struggling*, they are **looking in many different places for** / **thinking a lot about** / **trying very hard to do** something. (par. 6)

4. Something that is *urgent* is very **funny** / **important** / **sad**. (par. 7)

5. When you *pull over*, you **drive to the side of the road** / **move something toward you** / **talk fast**. (par. 7)

6. When there is something you want to *keep in mind*, you want to **hear** / **remember** / **study** it. (par. 8)

C Recognizing Point of View

> Sometimes a writer expresses a point of view, or an opinion. An important part of reading critically is the ability to recognize if the writer has expressed a point of view and if so, to understand what that point of view is.

Check (✓) the statement that best expresses the writer's point of view. Compare your answers with a partner.

_____ 1. People have to get used to others using their cell phones in public.

_____ 2. People should not complain when others use their cell phones in public.

_____ 3. There are some rules we should follow when we use cell phones in public.

_____ 4. There should be laws against using cell phones in some public places.

D Relating Reading to Personal Experience

Discuss these questions with your classmates.

1. What advice in the article do you agree with? What do you disagree with?

2. Where should cell phones be allowed? Where should they *not* be allowed?

3. How do you feel when someone interrupts a conversation with you to take a call? How do you feel about someone who texts while they are talking to you?

How Table Manners Became Polite

Thinking About What You Know

Check (✓) the rules of table manners that are polite in your culture. Compare your answers with a partner.

_____ 1. You should sit up straight.

_____ 2. You should keep your elbows off the table.

_____ 3. It's rude to look at someone else who is eating.

_____ 4. You should only use your right hand to eat.

_____ 5. You should not speak with a mouth full of food.

_____ 6. You should not pick your teeth.

_____ 7. You should use a napkin to wipe your hands.

_____ 8. You should say "please" and "thank you."

Skimming

Skim the reading to find and circle the table manners listed above. See what the writer says about each one. Then read the whole text.

Do you remember being told to sit up straight and keep your elbows off the table when you are eating? Well if you do, be grateful you weren't a child of America's early settlers. Back then, children weren't even allowed to sit at the table. They stood behind the adults and ate whatever the adults gave them. 1

Later, children were allowed to sit at the table, but they couldn't speak unless an adult spoke to them. They couldn't ask for a dish, either. They had to wait until an adult offered it to them. It was also considered rude to fidget, sing, or look at someone else who was eating. 2

Table manners are even older than tables. About 9,000 years ago, people cooked soups in pots. When they ate, they dipped spoons, made of wood or bone, into the cooking pot. The first rules of table manners determined who could dip into the pot first. Sometimes people didn't use spoons. They just picked out pieces of meat with their fingers. 3

Eating with the fingers has never disappeared. Some cultures still follow this custom. For example, some people use only the first three fingers of the right hand. In northern India, some 4 diners use only the fingertips of the right hand, but in the south, it is acceptable to use both hands. Far more people in the world eat with fingers (or chopsticks) than use forks and spoons. But everyone has rules about eating politely.

5   Table manners became quite important in Europe in the 1100s. That's when people developed the idea of courtesy, or how to behave in the court.[1] Soon rules about eating began appearing in written texts.

6   The rules were meant to make the dining experience pleasant and tidy. People had to keep their elbows down and not speak with their mouths full. Polite eaters did not pick their teeth with knives, and they weren't greedy.

7   In those days, there were no regular dining tables. At mealtimes, people set wooden boards on supports and covered them with cloth. That's where the expression "setting the table" comes from. At festival dinners, there were no individual plates, only large serving plates. Two people shared each soup bowl, and they used squares of stale bread as plates. After the meal, these squares of bread were given to the poor.

8   In the 1300s, the Renaissance[2] arrived in Europe. So did the fork. As new table customs developed, people began to eat from plates, and everyone had their own cup. People had to wipe their fingers on napkins, not the tablecloth. People couldn't throw bones on the floor anymore. It was more polite to leave them on the plate.

9   Nowadays people use many simple table manners without thinking. You probably say "please" and "thank you," and ask people to pass food to you, instead of reaching over everyone for it.

10   There are many other rules, especially at formal parties. One rule, for example, is about using the correct fork. If you're a guest, and you're not sure what to do, just do what the host does. Even if you use the wrong fork, you will be following the basic principle of table manners: Be thoughtful of others, and make dining as pleasant as possible.

---

[1] **court:** an official place where kings and queens live

[2] **Renaissance:** the period from the fourteenth into the seventeenth centuries in Europe when there were many artistic developments and new ideas

Adapted from *The Christian Science Monitor*

A Comprehension Check

Check (✓) the statement that best expresses the topic of the reading.

_____ 1. table manners at formal meals

_____ 2. the rules of eating around the world

_____ 3. the history of table manners

_____ 4. the reasons for modern table manners

B Vocabulary Study

Find the words in the box in the reading. Then complete the sentences.

fidget (par. 2)	dipped (par. 3)	picked out (par. 3)
greedy (par. 6)	stale (par. 7)	wipe (par. 8)

1. When I was a child, I always _____ my cookies in milk.

2. Yesterday's bread is _____. Please buy some fresh bread.

3. Please _____ your feet on the mat before you come into the house.

4. Don't _____ so much. Sit still.

5. Gustav _____ the vegetables from his soup because he doesn't like them.

6. She wanted to have more ice cream, but she was afraid her friends would think she was _____.

C Making Inferences

> Sometimes the reader must infer, or figure out, what the writer did not explain or state directly in the text.

Check (✓) the statements that you can infer from the reading. Compare your answers with a partner.

_____ 1. Children had a hard life in early America.

_____ 2. Children in early America were often hungry.

_____ 3. People did not use forks before the Renaissance.

_____ 4. If parents do not teach children table manners, children do not learn them.

_____ 5. In Europe, table manners were not very important before the 1100s.

_____ 6. There are rules for using certain forks at dinner parties today.

D Relating Reading to Personal Experience

Discuss these questions with your classmates.

1. How important are table manners? Do you think people should be able to eat any way they want?

2. Do other people's table manners sometimes bother you? If so, which ones?

3. Do you like people less when they have poor table manners? Why or why not?

Dinner with My Parents

Predicting

Read the information below. Then discuss with a partner what you think will happen in the reading. Check (✓) your answer.

In this excerpt from The Joy Luck Club, *Waverly takes her American boyfriend, Rich, to meet her parents. Waverly's parents were born in China, but they live in California.*

_____ 1. Waverly's parents' table manners will surprise Rich.

_____ 2. Waverly's parents and Rich will talk about the differences between American and Chinese table manners.

_____ 3. Waverly's parents will think that Rich's behavior is rude.

Skimming

Skim the reading to check your prediction. Then read the whole text.

1   I couldn't save Rich in the kitchen. And I couldn't save him later at the dinner table.

2   When I offered Rich a fork, he insisted on using his slippery ivory chopsticks. He held them splayed like the knock-kneed legs of an ostrich while picking up a large chunk of sauce-coated eggplant. Halfway between his plate and his open mouth, the chunk fell on his crisp white shirt. It took several minutes to get Shoshana to stop shrieking with laughter.

And then he had helped himself to big portions of the shrimp and snow peas, not realizing he should have taken only a polite spoonful, until everybody had had a morsel.   3

He had declined the sautéed new greens, the tender and expensive leaves of bean plants plucked before the sprouts turn into beans. And Shoshana refused to eat them also, pointing to Rich: "He didn't eat them! He didn't eat them!"   4

He thought he was being polite by refusing seconds, when he should have followed my father's example, who made a big show of taking small portions of seconds, thirds, and even fourths, always saying he could not resist another bite of something or other, and then groaning that he was so full he thought he would burst.   5

But the worst was when Rich criticized my mother's cooking, and he didn't even know what he had done. As is the Chinese cook's custom, my mother always made disparaging remarks about her own cooking. That night she chose to direct it toward her famous steamed pork and preserved vegetable dish, which she always served with special pride.   6

"Ai! This dish not salty enough, no flavor," she complained, after tasting a small bit. "It is too bad to eat."   7

This was our family's cue to eat some and proclaim it the best she had ever made. But before we could do so, Rich said, "You know, all it needs is a little soy sauce." And he proceeded to pour a riverful of the salty black stuff on the platter, right before my mother's horrified eyes.   8

And even though I was hoping throughout the dinner that my mother would somehow see Rich's kindness, his sense of humor and boyish charm, I knew he had failed miserably in her eyes.   9

From *The Joy Luck Club*

A Comprehension Check

Check (✓) the statements that describe Chinese table manners according to the reading.

_____ 1. You should try a little of everything on the table.

_____ 2. You can hold chopsticks any way you want to.

_____ 3. If you don't like something, you don't have to eat it.

_____ 4. If you really like something, you should take a large portion of it.

_____ 5. You should never eat more than two portions of anything.

_____ 6. The cook should never praise his or her own cooking.

_____ 7. You should never say you have eaten too much.

_____ 8. You should always praise the cook.

B Vocabulary Study

Find the words in the reading that match these definitions.

1. difficult to hold _____ (par. 2)

2. a piece of something _____ (par. 2)

3. covered with a thin amount of something _____ (par. 2)

4. crying out loudly _____ (par. 2)

5. explode _____ (par. 5)

6. said that something was bad _____ (par. 6)

7. insulting _____ (par. 6)

8. state or announce _____ (par. 8)

C Paraphrasing

> Paraphrasing means using your own words to say what you have read. This is one strategy you can use to improve your understanding of a text.

Circle the letter of the correct paraphrase for each paragraph.

1. Paragraph 3
   a. He should have eaten his food after everyone else had gotten some.
   b. He shouldn't have taken a lot to eat before everyone had some.

2. Paragraph 5
   a. He didn't realize it was polite to keep taking food while insisting he couldn't eat more.
   b. He watched my father eat a lot and then feel ill, so he refused more food.

3. Paragraph 9
   a. There were a lot of good things about Rich, but my mother didn't see them.
   b. I wanted my mother and Rich to like each other, but I could see that they didn't.

D Relating Reading to Personal Experience

Discuss these questions with your classmates.

> Reread one of the unit readings and time yourself. Note your reading speed in the chart on page 124.

1. What do you think Waverly and Rich said about the dinner the next day? How about Waverly's parents?

2. Do you think Rich should apologize to Waverly's parents? Why or why not?

3. Have you ever been embarrassed because you realized that you used the wrong table manners? If so, describe the situation.

Fear

Look at the titles of the readings and their brief descriptions to preview this unit's content. Before you begin each reading, answer the questions about it.

Reading 1

Flying? No Fear

Fear of flying is more common than you may think. This newspaper article describes a class that people take to help them overcome their fear of flying.

1. What do you like most about traveling by plane? What do you like least?

2. Are you afraid of flying? If so, what causes you the greatest worry – takeoff, landing, unusual noises, or turbulence?

3. How do you think people should deal with their fear during a flight?

Reading 2

Don't Fight a Good Fright

Why do people enjoy fantasy frights, such as horror movies or haunted houses? In this article, the writer offers some explanations for our love of fear.

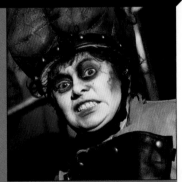

1. What kinds of things scare you?

2. Do you enjoy watching horror movies, going to haunted houses, or going on scary rides at an amusement park? Why or why not?

3. Do you think it is harmful to experience brief moments of intense fear? Why or why not?

Reading 3

Stage Fright

Some professional performers suffer greatly from stage fright. This newspaper article explains some strategies they can learn for dealing with their fear.

1. How do you think professional singers and musicians feel before a performance?

2. Who is your favorite singer or musician? Does this performer look confident or nervous at a performance?

3. Do you think people can learn to be less nervous before a performance? If so, what strategies can you suggest?

Flying? No Fear

Thinking About the Topic

Imagine that you are afraid of flying and that you take a class to overcome your fear. Check (✓) the things that you would want to have included in the class. Compare your answers with a partner.

_____ 1. A pilot explains how an airplane flies.

_____ 2. A speaker explains how airplanes deal with turbulence.

_____ 3. A psychologist tells you how to stop imagining disasters.

_____ 4. You take a short flight.

_____ 5. You spend some time with the pilots.

Skimming

Skim the reading to see which of the things the fear-of-flying class includes. Then read the whole text.

1   Fear of flying is a common problem. One study claims that 20 percent of us feel terrified about airplane flight. Is it possible that taking a class could help?

2   I am sitting with my wife, who is afraid to fly, and 120 strangers in a hotel near a busy airport. Dr. Keith Stoll, a psychologist, and 15 other experts are taking us through a one-day fear-of-flying class.

3   In the morning, our fears are addressed. Pilot Richard Parkinson gives a clear explanation of how an airplane flies, and talks about the parts of a flight that cause the most anxiety. Turbulence, or sudden movements of the plane, is the biggest trigger. It's uncomfortable, but common, and Parkinson explains how planes are built to deal with it.

The afternoon session deals with psychological issues. Fear of flying, like many other phobias, is marked by "catastrophizing" – obsessively thinking about disasters. The simplest solution, says Stoll, involves mental discipline: Simply stop yourself. The moment you find yourself picturing the worst, think about something more pleasant. If you do it often enough, the habit will weaken.   4

At the back of everyone's minds is the 40-minute flight at the end of the day. The question is, who will get on the plane? There are different levels of anxiety in the group. Some people are simply nervous, others very frightened. Georgina Chapman is somewhere in the middle. She has flown many times, but her fear has grown with each trip. It's a surprisingly common problem: People remember every moment of uneasiness during years of flying, but they forget the peaceful trips. As a result, they expect the worst.   5

"I went to Bali and spent two weeks lying on the beach," says Georgina. "It sounds like fun, but it wasn't. I spent the whole time looking up at the planes, terrified at the thought I'd have to get on one to get home."   6

This is the second class for David Green: The first time he couldn't leave the hotel for the airport. He's a big man, reluctant to show fear, but his hands are white. "I want to go to Majorca for a vacation with my family, but right now I just can't," he says. "The worst thing is, I think I'm starting to communicate my fear to my son."   7

Toward the end of the afternoon, the tension is rising. It's almost time for the flight. My wife is pale, but relatively calm. It's hard for some of the other people to overcome their fear. A few won't even leave the hotel. David Green nervously walks to the plane, walks back, boards again.   8

The flight is strange. People show a variety of emotions in the cabin. First-time fliers happily wonder why they had worried, and experienced fliers smile nervously and talk about the reduction in their anxiety. Here and there, a tearful passenger is having a terrible panic attack. Everyone is invited to spend a minute with the pilots. They make a point of informing passengers of the reason for every thump, clunk, and patch of turbulence.   9

When we land, most passengers are smiling. Georgina Chapman is happy: "It has definitely helped. I was much more comfortable." David Green stepped on and off the plane one time too many – and stayed in the boarding area. "Next time," he says. "Next time I'll go." I hope he does. He looks like a man who needs a vacation.   10

Adapted from *The Sunday Times*

A Comprehension Check

Complete each sentence with *All, None, One,* or *Some*.

1. _____ of the class participants had a fear of flying.

2. _____ of them had taken a fear of flying class before.

3. _____ of them had flown before.

4. _____ of them got on a plane at the beginning of the class.

5. _____ of them took a short flight at the end of the class.

6. _____ of them succeeded in overcoming their fear of flying.

B Vocabulary Study

Find the words in the box in the reading. Then write the words next to their definitions.

trigger (*n.*) (par. 3)	anxiety (pars. 3, 5, 9)	obsessively (par. 4)
phobias (par. 4)	patch (*n.*) (par. 9)	land (*v.*) (par. 10)

1. arrive at a place after traveling by air or sea _____

2. without being able to stop doing something _____

3. a feeling of worry or nervousness _____

4. something that causes something else _____

5. a small area _____

6. extreme, powerful fears _____

C Recognizing Cause and Effect

> When you read, it is important to recognize the reason why something happens (the cause). It is also important to recognize what happens as a result (the effect).

Use the information in the reading to decide whether each statement below is a cause or an effect of fear of flying. Write *C* (cause) or *E* (effect).

_____ 1. You feel the sudden movement of the plane.

_____ 2. You worry about flying home during your vacation.

_____ 3. Your skin turns a pale color.

_____ 4. You don't understand how planes stay in the air.

_____ 5. You have just seen a movie about a terrible plane crash.

_____ 6. You have a panic attack on the plane.

D Relating Reading to Personal Experience

Discuss these questions with your classmates.

1. Would you recommend that someone with a fear of flying take a class like the one described in the reading? Why or why not?

2. Have you ever had a bad experience on a plane? If so, what happened?

3. Do you have any phobias, such as a fear of heights or elevators? If so, how do you deal with these fears?

Don't Fight a Good Fright

Predicting

Look at the title and the pictures. Check (✓) the statement you think the writer will agree with. Compare your answers with a partner.

_____ 1. People who are fearful should not go to horror movies.

_____ 2. People should avoid things that frighten them so that they don't get hurt.

_____ 3. People can enjoy something frightening when they know nothing bad will happen.

_____ 4. People who are fearful must learn to handle their fear by going to haunted houses or taking thrill rides at amusement parks.

Skimming

Skim the text to check your prediction. Then read the whole text.

Mark DeMatteis had just paid money to walk past creepy clowns and a screaming madman with a chainsaw, and he was enjoying every minute of it. "I love to be scared. I love the art of it," he said. DeMatteis is a connoisseur of haunted houses and horror movies. He's never experienced a fantasy fright that he didn't like. The key word for DeMatteis is fantasy. He says he prefers experiencing that kind of fright to the real thing. 1

There's no doubt that real life can be scary sometimes, or even dangerous to one's health. That is evidently part of the reason people love a good fright in a haunted house or movie theater, where they can manage the fear with little actual risk involved. 2

"It's gratifying for people to face something that resembles something they're really scared of, and be able to say, 'I did it, I controlled it, I didn't fall apart,'" said Glenn Sparks, a university professor who has studied how people handle frightening images in the media. 3

4   Sparks has observed how haunted houses and horror films are common dating experiences for young couples. He believes that males and females have expectations of how the other should act. "If a male goes into one of those situations and expresses mastery and control, females tend to find him more attractive and he is admired more," he said. "Similarly, for a female, the normal reaction is to show fear. If a female doesn't show that, the female becomes less attractive." When asked who reacts the most in haunted houses, DeMatteis supported the theory. "Young women 16 to 30 are the main ones that scream, without a doubt."

5   Fantasy fright is rarely harmful to the body; however, DeMatteis recalled that a man once collapsed inside a haunted house, but he recovered. Coroner[1] Cyril Wecht is unaware of any cases in which people reacted to frightening images so strongly that they were literally scared to death. However, he doesn't rule out the possibility. It depends on the strength of the person's heart at the time he experiences intense fear. Dr. Wecht and others say that a real-life fear is much more likely to affect one's health than deliberate exposure to frightening settings.

6   Social worker Jerilyn Ross says that for most people, a certain level of fear and anxiety and scaring yourself is kind of exciting. Consider Theresa Streshenkoff's experience. She was on her third trip to the haunted house even though she said she's easily scared. Her first time, she ran screaming from a frightening figure in costume. She still felt a thrill going through the house again days later, even after she knew what to expect. "It isn't supposed to be fun to be scared, but if it's frightening and you know it's not going to hurt you, it's fun," she explained.

---

[1] **coroner:** an official who examines the causes of a person's death, especially if it was unexpected

Adapted from *Pittsburgh Post-Gazette*

A Comprehension Check

Write the number of the paragraph that answers each question.

_____ a. What is part of the reason why people like scary experiences?

_____ b. How often are people physically hurt by fright?

_____ c. How does Theresa Streshenkoff feel about haunted houses?

_____ d. How does Mark DeMatteis feel about haunted houses and horror movies?

_____ e. Why do young couples go to scary movies or haunted houses on dates?

_____ f. Why do people feel happy when they deal with their fear?

B Vocabulary Study

Find the words and phrases in *italics* in the reading. Then circle the correct meanings.

1. Something *creepy* is frightening because it is **amusing / new / strange**. (par. 1)

2. Someone who is a *connoisseur* is **a clown / an expert / a young man**. (par. 1)

3. A *fantasy* is something exciting that you **do / fear / imagine**. (par. 1)

4. Something that is *gratifying* makes people feel **brave / frightened / satisfied**. (par. 3)

5. When people are *literally scared to death*, they **die / look sick / show fear**. (par. 5)

6. When you *rule out* something, you decide that it is **impossible / scary / true**. (par. 5)

7. Something that is *deliberate* happens **accidentally / often / on purpose**. (par. 5)

C Making Inferences

> Sometimes the reader must infer, or figure out, what the writer did not explain or state directly in the text.

Check (✓) the statements that you can infer from the reading.

_____ 1. Mark DeMatteis has never been afraid.

_____ 2. People like to feel that they can control their fears.

_____ 3. People go on scary amusement park rides to prove that they are brave.

_____ 4. Teenage boys who show they are afraid won't have a lot of girlfriends.

_____ 5. Someone who has a weak heart should never go to haunted houses.

_____ 6. Theresa Streshenkoff will go to haunted houses in the future.

D Relating Reading to Personal Experience

Discuss these questions with your classmates.

1. What is the last scary movie you saw? Which parts were the most frightening? How did you react during the scary parts?

2. Do you think it's fun to do scary things when you know they are not going to hurt you?

3. The writer says that females find males who don't show fear more attractive. Do you agree? Do you think males find females who don't show fear less attractive? Explain your answer.

Stage Fright

Previewing Vocabulary

Look at the picture, the title, and the words and phrases from the reading in the box. Discuss their meanings with a partner. Look up any new words in a dictionary.

blank mind	fall down	icy fingers	jittery	onstage
panic	racing heart	scared to death	shaky limbs	throbbing

Scanning

Scan the reading to find and circle the words and phrases from the box. Discuss how you think they relate to the topic of the reading. Then read the whole text.

1 Fall down as you come onstage. That's an odd trick. Not recommended. But it saved the pianist Vladimir Feltsman when he was a teenager back in Moscow. The veteran cellist Mstislav Rostropovich tripped him purposely to cure him of pre-performance panic, Mr. Feltsman said, "All my fright was gone. I already fell. What else could happen?"

2 Today, music schools are addressing the problem of anxiety in classes that deal with performance techniques and career preparation. There are a variety of strategies that musicians can learn to fight stage fright and its symptoms: icy fingers, shaky limbs, racing heart, blank mind.

3 Teachers and psychologists offer wide-ranging advice, from basics like learning pieces inside out, to mental discipline, such as visualizing a performance and taking steps to relax. Don't deny that you're jittery, they urge; some excitement is natural, even necessary for dynamic playing. And play in public often, simply for the experience.

Psychotherapist Diane Nichols suggests some strategies for the moments before performance, "Take two deep abdominal breaths, open up your shoulders, then smile," she says. "And not one of these 'please don't kill me' smiles. Then choose three friendly faces in the audience, people you would communicate with and make music to, and make eye contact with them." She doesn't want performers to think of the audience as a judge. **4**

Extreme demands by mentors or parents are often at the root of stage fright, says Dorothy DeLay, a well-known violin teacher. She tells other teachers to demand only what their students are able to achieve. **5**

When Lynn Harrell was 20, he became the principal cellist of the Cleveland Orchestra, and he suffered extreme stage fright. "There were times when I got so nervous I was sure the audience could see my chest responding to the throbbing. It was just total panic. I came to a point where I thought, 'If I have to go through this to play music, I think I'm going to look for another job.'" Recovery, he said, involved developing humility – recognizing that whatever his talent, he was fallible, and that an imperfect concert was not a disaster. **6**

It is not only young artists who suffer, of course. The legendary pianist Vladimir Horowitz's nerves were famous. The great tenor Franco Corelli is another example. "They had to push him on stage," soprano Renata Scotto recalled. **7**

Actually, success can make things worse. "In the beginning of your career, when you're scared to death, nobody knows who you are, and they don't have any expectations," soprano June Anderson said. "There's less to lose. Later on, when you're known, people are coming to see you, and they have certain expectations. You have a lot to lose." **8**

Anderson added, "I never stop being nervous until I've sung my last note." **9**

Adapted from *The New York Times*

A Comprehension Check

Mark each statement *T* (true) or *F* (false). Then correct the false statements.

_F_ 1. Falling down onstage was ~~not~~ a good way for the pianist Vladimir Feltsman to deal with his stage fright.

_____ 2. There are many signs of stage fright.

_____ 3. Teachers and psychologists cannot help people with extreme stage fright.

_____ 4. To perform well on stage, you need to have some feelings of excitement.

_____ 5. If you have stage fright, it's helpful to make eye contact with people in the audience who look friendly.

_____ 6. Often people have stage fright because parents or teachers expect too much of them.

_____ 7. Famous musicians never suffer from stage fright.

_____ 8. Famous musicians do not have to worry about performing well.

B Vocabulary Study

Find the words in the box in the reading. Then complete the sentences.

tripped (par. 1)	symptoms (par. 2)	wide-ranging (par. 3)
visualizing (par. 3)	mentors (par. 5)	fallible (par. 6)

1. A rapidly beating heart and cold hands are common _____ of stage fright.

2. Your _____ teach you and give you a lot of valuable career advice.

3. We are all _____. Everybody makes mistakes.

4. I didn't see the step, so I _____ and fell.

5. Her musical interests are _____. She loves all kinds of music.

6. Imagine yourself playing the piano before an audience. _____ a performance will help you to feel less nervous.

C Understanding Text Organization

> In a well-organized text, related topics are grouped together and presented in a logical sequence. If you understand how a text is organized, it will be easier to understand the ideas.

Number the information about stage fright from _1_ to _6_ according to the order it is mentioned in the reading.

_____ a. people with stage fright

_____ b. an unusual experience with stage fright

_____ c. symptoms of stage fright

_____ d. possible cures for stage fright

_____ e. causes of stage fright

_____ f. the effects of success

D Relating Reading to Personal Experience

Discuss these questions with your classmates.

1. Have you ever spoken or performed in front of an audience? If so, was it a good experience? Why or why not?

2. Have you ever suffered from stage fright? If so, what were your symptoms?

3. What do you think is the most helpful piece of advice in the reading?

> Reread one of the unit readings and time yourself. Note your reading speed in the chart on page 124.

10 The Paranormal

Look at the titles of the readings and their brief descriptions to preview this unit's content. Before you begin each reading, answer the questions about it.

Reading 1

Psychic Solves Crimes

This newspaper article reveals how a psychic has provided the police with extremely useful help in solving crimes.

1. What methods do the police usually use to solve crimes?

2. What is a psychic? How do you think a psychic could help the police find criminals?

3. Do you think the police should use psychics to help them solve crimes? Why or why not?

Reading 2

A Near-Death Experience (NDE)

In this article from the Internet, you learn about the extraordinary feelings of people who have come close to dying.

1. What have you heard about people who had strange experiences when they were near death?

2. Do you believe that people can have out-of-body experiences, that is, feel as if they have left their bodies? Why or why not?

3. What kinds of visions do you think people might have when they are close to death?

Reading 3

Mind over Matter

Do you believe that the mind is more powerful than the body? This article explains how that idea is used to help people.

1. Do you believe in mind over matter? For example, do you believe that if you concentrate hard enough, you will not feel pain if you step into very hot water? Why or why not?

2. Have you heard about or seen people who are able to move inanimate objects just by staring at them? Give examples.

3. How strong is your power of concentration? Explain your answer.

Psychic Solves Crimes

Previewing Vocabulary

The words in the box are from the reading. Discuss the meanings of the words with a partner. Look up any new words in a dictionary.

cemetery	clues	investigations	murder
psychic	theft	strange	visions

Scanning

Scan the reading to find and circle the words from the box. Discuss how you think these words relate to the topic of the reading. Then read the whole text.

1   A psychic who secretly helped Scotland Yard[1] solve hundreds of crimes over more than 20 years spoke about her extraordinary relationship with the police. Nella Jones revealed details about a series of cases where her information led directly to the criminals. The Metropolitan Police, who had never publicly acknowledged her role, held a dinner in her honor to express gratitude for her "invaluable" help in catching a range of criminals.

2   Her relationship with the police began many years ago, shortly after the theft of Johannes Vermeer's painting *The Guitar Player* from a house in London. Ms. Jones soon began to receive visions, or "psychic clues," that told her the painting was in a cemetery in east London. The police found it, undamaged and wrapped in newspaper, in St. Bartholomew's churchyard. "After that, word got around, and it was not long before other police officers came to call, asking if I could help out," she said.

---

[1] *Scotland Yard:* the central police headquarters of the United Kingdom

Since then, she has helped solve various murders, forecast where bombs would be placed, and traced money stolen in bank robberies. "The sensations you feel are sometimes awful," she said. "You often pick up the pain of the victims. I sometimes think it's not a gift, but a curse." 3

Once Ms. Jones almost single-handedly solved a murder. Investigating officers took her to the room where someone had killed an old woman. She immediately ran out into the street, telling officers she could see the letters EARL and a red Cortina[2] with a rusty roof rack. There was a garage called Earl Motors on a nearby street. Investigations by police revealed that a man had recently sold the garage owners a red Cortina with a rusty roof rack. He turned out to be the man who had murdered the old woman. 4

"Nella has given invaluable assistance on a number of murders," said Detective Chief Inspector Arnie Cooke, "We have to keep an open mind to the paranormal. It would be stupid not to follow up the leads she gives us. There are a lot of strange things happening." 5

Ms. Jones says everyone is born with abilities similar to hers, but few try to use them. "It's the most natural thing in the world." Ms. Jones believes, however, that her days of helping the police – for which she never received any money – are over. "I'm getting too old," she said. "I have seen and felt some terrible things. I don't even want to think about them now. Sometimes I think I've done my bit for society." 6

---

[2] **Cortina:** a kind of car

Adapted from *Sunday Telegraph*

A Comprehension Check

Find and correct the four mistakes in each police report. The first one has been corrected for you.

1. Ms. Jones came to help us ~~before~~ *after* the theft of *The Guitar Player*, painted by Johannes Vermeer. She began to have visions about the painting. She saw that it was in a house in west London. We went to look for it and found it. The story was in a newspaper.

2. There was a murder. Someone had killed an old man. We took Ms. Jones to the street where the murder took place. She had a vision of the letters CAR and a red Cortina. We found out that a man had recently bought a red car at a garage called Earl Motors. The man was the murderer.

B Vocabulary Study

Find the words in *italics* in the reading. Then match the words with their meanings.

_____ 1. *invaluable* (par. 1 & 5)   a. covered with a reddish-brownish substance

_____ 2. *gratitude* (par. 1)   b. alone, without help

_____ 3. *forecast* (par. 3)   c. something bad

_____ 4. *curse* (par. 3)   d. extremely useful

_____ 5. *single-handedly* (par. 4)   e. thankfulness

_____ 6. *rusty* (par. 4)   f. predicted

C Making Inferences

> Sometimes the reader must infer, or figure out, what the writer did not explain or state directly in the text.

Check (✓) the statements that you can infer from the reading.

_____ 1. Ms. Jones likes to help people.

_____ 2. Ms. Jones would continue to help the police if they paid her.

_____ 3. Ms. Jones sometimes wishes she didn't have psychic powers.

_____ 4. Thieves took *The Guitar Player* to the cemetery because they wanted to hide it.

_____ 5. Detective Cooke would follow leads from other people with psychic powers.

_____ 6. Other psychics have also helped Detective Cooke solve crimes.

_____ 7. Ms. Jones is going to die soon.

D Relating Reading to Personal Experience

Discuss these questions with your classmates.

1. Do you agree that everyone is born with psychic abilities, but few try to use them? Do you think these powers are a gift or a curse?

2. Do you think you have psychic powers? If so, what visions have you had? If not, would you want to have this ability?

3. In what other ways could someone's psychic powers be useful to society?

A Near-Death Experience (NDE)

Thinking About the Topic

Read the experiences listed below. Check (✓) the ones you think people have during near-death experiences. Compare your answers with a partner.

_____ 1. feeling that you have left your body

_____ 2. feeling that you are moving through a dark space or tunnel

_____ 3. encountering dead loved ones

_____ 4. experiencing events in your future life

_____ 5. having the feeling that you do not understand anything

_____ 6. seeing a strong, bright light

Skimming

Skim the reading to see which experiences the writer discusses. Then read the whole text.

Most people who have come close to death say they remember nothing. Sometimes, however, people report what we now call a "near-death experience" (NDE) – a term that was first coined by Dr. Raymond Moody in 1975. It may be that more people are reporting such experiences in modern times because medical science is making it possible to bring more people back from near death. In addition to people who have almost died, there are others who have had similar experiences. They have reported NDEs while meditating, experiencing grief, or even just going about their daily lives. Whatever the reason for it, an NDE is among the most powerful experiences that a person can have. It may permanently change a person's perception of what is real and important. 1

One extraordinary aspect of NDEs is that a person's age, culture, religion, race, or education does not affect the features of the experience. The way people describe the NDE, however, varies according to their background and language ability. 2

3   Most NDEs are pleasant and joyful, but others can be very frightening. There is no evidence that the type of experience is related to whether the person is religious or not, or if the person has lived a "good" or "bad" life according to society's standards. Nonetheless, an NDE often strongly affects how people continue to live their lives.

4   No two NDEs are identical, but they always include one or more of the following:

- Feeling that the "self" has left the body and is overhead. The person experiencing the NDE may later be able to describe in great detail where he or she was, who else was there, and what happened.
- Moving through a dark space or tunnel
- Experiencing very powerful emotions, ranging from bliss to terror
- Encountering a brilliant light
- Receiving a message such as, "It is not yet your time."
- Meeting others, such as dead loved ones or unidentified "beings of light," which may be symbols from the person's own religious tradition or from other religious traditions
- Seeing and re-experiencing major events in the person's life
- Having a sense of understanding everything and knowing how the universe works
- Reaching a boundary – a cliff, fence, water, or some kind of barrier that the person may not cross without losing the ability to return to life
- Deciding to return to life, either voluntarily or involuntarily. If the return is voluntary, it is usually linked to relationships with living people.
- Returning to the body

5   No one knows why some people experience NDEs and others do not. And researchers don't know why most people report pleasurable experiences. What we do know is that an NDE can change a person's life dramatically.

Adapted from www.iands.org/nde.html

A Comprehension Check

Mark each statement _T_ (true) or _F_ (false). Then correct the false statements.

_F_ 1. ~~Most~~ *Some* people who come close to death will have a near-death experience.

____ 2. People who do not come close to death can have a near-death experience.

____ 3. The characteristics of a near-death experience vary according to a person's culture.

____ 4. Some people enjoy their near-death experience.

____ 5. Two different people can have exactly the same near-death experiences.

____ 6. Near-death experiences can involve visions or a sense of physical movement.

____ 7. After a near-death experience, people's lives can change.

____ 8. Researchers know why some people have NDEs and others do not.

B Vocabulary Study

Find the words in the box in the reading. Then write the words next to their definitions.

coined (par. 1)	perception (par. 1)	background (par. 2)
bliss (par. 4)	brilliant (par. 4)	voluntary (par. 4)

1. the things that have made you into the person you are, especially family, experience, and education   _____

2. extreme happiness   _____

3. used for the first time   _____

4. awareness and understanding   _____

5. done freely, by choice rather than by force   _____

6. very strong and bright   _____

C Recognizing Purpose

> Writers create texts for different purposes. For example, sometimes a writer wants to give information. Other times, the writer wants to persuade the reader to do something. Recognizing a writer's purpose will help you better understand what you read.

Check (✓) the writer's main purpose in the reading. Discuss the reasons for your answer with a partner.

_____ 1. to persuade people that near-death experiences are real

_____ 2. to compare different types of near-death experiences

_____ 3. to give people information about near-death experiences

D Relating Reading to Personal Experience

Discuss these questions with your classmates.

1. Do you believe that people who come close to dying have similar experiences to the ones described in the reading? Why or why not?

2. Have you ever dreamed about a loved one who has died? If so, what do you remember about the dream?

3. Have you ever had an experience that changed your life? If so, what happened?

Mind over Matter

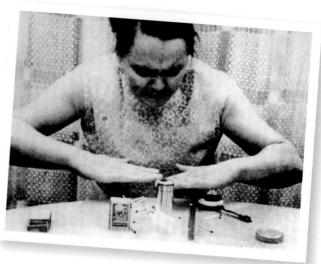

Nina Kulagina

Thinking About What You Know

How much do you know about the power of the mind? Look at the title and the pictures. Then check (✓) the statements you think are true. Compare your answers with a partner.

_____ 1. Some people claim that they can move objects with just their thoughts.

_____ 2. Today everyone agrees that telekinesis (the ability to move objects with your mind) is possible.

_____ 3. Scientific experiments prove that anyone can learn to practice telekinesis.

_____ 4. Medical scientists believe that someday computer chips placed in the brains of paralyzed people will allow them to move by using their thoughts.

Skimming

Skim the reading to see which of the statements are true. Then read the whole text.

1   Nina Kulagina was sitting at a table in a quiet room. She was trying hard to clear her mind and focus her attention on the drinking glass in front of her. She stared at the glass for a long time, but she didn't touch it. All of a sudden, the glass began to move! Kulagina claimed that she could move inanimate objects with the power of her mind alone. This ability is called telekinesis. Some people refer to it as "mind over matter."

2   Kulagina was famous for her amazing mental powers. Films made during her life in Russia (1926–1990) show her accomplishing such feats as moving the needles of a compass, raising a ping-pong ball into the air, and even separating the white from the yolk of an egg! Did Kulagina actually move these objects with just her mind? Telekinesis is a controversial subject. Some people believe in it; others do not.

3   Many believers say that even ordinary people can learn telekinesis by doing exercises that involve deep concentration. They often cite the Psi wheel experiment as proof. A Psi wheel is a device made of a small piece of paper shaped like a pyramid that balances on the tip of a pointed object such as a needle. One way to do the experiment is to sit a short distance from the Psi wheel, extend the hands toward the device, and concentrate

intensely on it. The Psi wheel may start to spin. Believers in telekinesis say the movement is caused by waves of mental energy.

Skeptics, however, say that the movement results from heat from the person's hands, 4 which causes the air to warm and rise, thus moving the wheel. Skeptics believe that there is always a scientific explanation for the movement of inanimate objects. Most scientists agree. They believe that telekinesis experiments are not properly set up or controlled.

Surprisingly, recent advances in medical science suggest that it may indeed be possible to 5 control objects with our minds. In order to help paralyzed people, scientists have developed a tiny computer chip that can be placed inside a person's brain. The chip is then connected via wires to a computer to which the person sends mental commands. Using these commands, the person is able to control the movement of objects such as an artificial arm. In this way, a paralyzed person would be able to move the arm just by thinking about it.

Scientists are now working on the development of a smaller, wireless version of the 6 chip, so that a direct connection between the person and a computer will no longer be needed. This type of chip would be placed in the brain and it would allow the person to communicate wirelessly with a computer worn on a belt.

Scientists believe that one day it will be 7 possible to connect the chip in the brain with a system of electronic stimulators that are plugged directly into the muscles of a person's arms and legs. It is their hope that in the future, the chip will enable paralyzed people to have full mobility. The rapid progress of the research and the plans for the future clearly demonstrate how "mind over matter" has become a reality in the world of medical science.

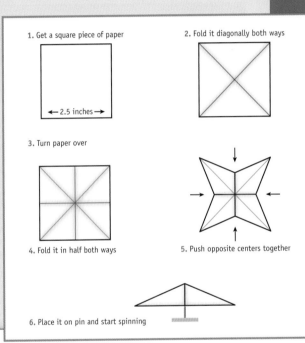

How to make a Psi wheel

A Comprehension Check

Check (✓) the four main topics of the reading.

_____ 1. Nina Kulagina's ability to move things with her mind

_____ 2. Nina Kulagina's ability to move a glass just by staring at it

_____ 3. what those who believe in telekinesis say

_____ 4. what a Psi wheel is

_____ 5. what those who do not believe in telekinesis say

_____ 6. how telekinesis is being used in medical developments

_____ 7. computer chips in the brains of paralyzed people

_____ 8. wireless communication between computer chips in people's brains and computers people wear on belts

B Vocabulary Study

Find the words in *italics* in the reading. Then match the words with their meanings.

_____ 1. *feats* (par. 2)   a. people who doubt something is true

_____ 2. *device* (par. 3)   b. objects used to make something active

_____ 3. *spin* (par. 3)   c. an object invented for a specific purpose

_____ 4. *skeptics* (par. 4)   d. ability to move

_____ 5. *stimulators* (par. 7)   e. great accomplishments

_____ 6. *mobility* (par. 7)   f. turn around and around

C Recognizing Cause and Effect

> When you read, it is important to recognize the reason why something happens (cause). It is also important to recognize what happens as a result (effect).

Match the causes and effects according to the reading. Write the letter of the correct effect for each cause.

a. paralyzed people have full mobility	c. glass began to move
b. wheel may start to spin	d. control movement of objects

Cause		Effect
1. stared at the glass for a long time (par. 1)	→	_____
2. sit a short distance from the Psi wheel, extend hands toward the device, and concentrate intensely (par. 3)	→	_____
3. computer chip is placed inside a person's brain (par. 5)	→	_____
4. stimulators plugged directly into a person's muscles (par. 7)	→	_____

D Relating Reading to Personal Experience

Discuss these questions with your classmates.

1. If you had the power of telekinesis, how would you use it in your daily life?

2. Can you think of how wireless chips could be used in the brains of healthy people? What could they be used for?

3. Is it useful for scientists to do research on the paranormal? Why or why not?

> Reread one of the unit readings and time yourself. Note your reading speed in the chart on page 124.

Languages

Look at the titles of the readings and their brief descriptions to preview this unit's content. Before you begin each reading, answer the questions about it.

Reading 1 ▶ ## The Day a Language Died

In this article, you learn about the last speaker of a Native American language and what the death of a language means for humanity.

1. What are some examples of countries where many different languages are spoken?

2. Why do you think some languages become more powerful than other languages?

3. Is it better if everyone in a country speaks the same language? Why or why not?

Reading 2 ▶ ## Aping Language

This magazine article explores the question of whether apes can understand and produce language.

1. How do animals communicate? Give some examples.

2. Do you think animals can understand human language? Why or why not?

3. Why do you think researchers often use chimps to study language in animals?

Reading 3 ▶ ## The Bilingual Brain

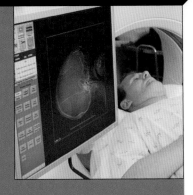

The writer of this article discusses the parts of the brain that play a role in language learning by people of different ages.

1. What is the best age to start learning another language? Why do you think so?

2. Why is it easier for some people to learn a new language than it is for others?

3. What is the easiest part of learning a second language for you? What is the hardest part?

The Day a Language Died

Thinking About the Topic

Answer these questions with a partner.

1. How many languages do you think are spoken in the world?
   a. about 300   b. about 6,000   c. about 10,000

2. What are the most widely spoken languages in the world?
   a. English, Spanish, Chinese
   b. French, Arabic, Portuguese
   c. Japanese, Hindi, Russian

3. How many languages do you think are in danger of dying out?
   a. about 200   b. about 1,500   c. about 3,000

Carlos Westez

Scanning

Scan the reading to find the answers to the questions. Then read the whole text.

1   When Carlos Westez died at the age of 76, a language died, too. Westez, more commonly known as Red Thunder Cloud, was the last speaker of the Native American language, Catawba.

2   Anyone who wants to hear various songs of the Catawba can contact the Smithsonian Institution in Washington, D.C., where, back in the 1940s, Red Thunder Cloud recorded a series of songs for future generations. Some people might want to try to learn some of these songs by heart. They are all that is left of the Catawba language. The language that people used to speak is gone forever.

3   We are all aware of the damage that modern industry can do to the world's ecology.[1] However, few people are aware of the impact that widely spoken languages have on other languages and ways of life. English has spread all over the world. Chinese, Spanish, Russian, and Hindi have become powerful languages, as well. As these languages become more powerful, their use as tools of business and culture increases. When this happens, hundreds of languages that are spoken by only a few people die out.

---

[1] *ecology:* the relationship of living things to their environment and to each other

Scholars believe there are about 6,000 languages around the world, but more than half of them could die out within the next 100 years. There are many examples. Araki is a native language of the island of Vanuatu, located in the Pacific Ocean. It is spoken by only a few older adults, so like Catawba, Araki will soon disappear. Many languages of Ethiopia will have the same fate because each one has only a few speakers. Papua New Guinea is an extremely rich source of different languages, but more than 100 of them are in danger of extinction. In the Americas, 100 languages, each of which has fewer than 300 speakers, also are dying out.

4

Red Thunder Cloud was one of the first to recognize the threat of language death and to try to do something about it. He was not actually born into the Catawba tribe, and the language was not his mother tongue. However, he was a frequent visitor to the Catawba reservation[2] in South Carolina, where he learned the language. The songs he sang for the Smithsonian Institution helped to make Native American music popular. Now he is gone, and the language is dead.

5

What does it mean when a language disappears? When a plant or insect or animal species dies, it is easy to understand what we've lost and to appreciate what this means for the balance of the natural world. However, language is only a product of the mind. To be the last remaining speaker of a language, like Red Thunder Cloud, must be a lonely destiny, almost as strange and terrible as being the last surviving member of a dying species. For the rest of us, when a language dies, we lose the possibility of a unique way of seeing and describing the world.

6

[2] **reservation:** an area of land made available for a particular group of people to live in

Adapted from *The Independent*

A Comprehension Check

For each question, two of the answers are correct. Cross out the answer that is *not* correct.

1. What do we know about Red Thunder Cloud?
    a. His real name was Carlos Westez.
    b. He spoke the Catawba language, but he was not a native Catawba.
    c. He earned a living by singing Catawba songs.

2. What is true about the Catawba language?
    a. People still speak the language in South Carolina.
    b. Nobody speaks the language any more.
    c. You can listen to songs in the language.

3. Why do some languages disappear?
    a. Other languages become more powerful.
    b. Governments want everybody to speak one language.
    c. These languages don't have many native speakers.

4. What will happen to languages in the future?
    a. Thousands of languages will die out.
    b. Languages that are spoken by few people will probably disappear.
    c. There will be more languages in the future than in the past.

B Vocabulary Study

Find the words in the box in the reading. Then complete the sentences.

back (par. 2)	by heart (par. 2)	spread (par. 3)
extinction (par. 4)	species (par. 6)	destiny (par. 6)

1. I've heard the song so many times that I know it _____.

2. I took Spanish language classes _____ in high school.

3. People on the island believe it is their _____ to save the language.

4. This _____ of bird sings only in the evening. Most other kinds sing in the morning.

5. One way that languages _____ around the world is through movies.

6. We often think of plants and animals in danger of _____. This is also true of many languages.

C Making Inferences

> Sometimes the reader must infer, or figure out, what the writer did not explain or state directly in the text.

Check (✓) the statements that you can infer from the reading.

_____ 1. A language that is not used in business is more likely to disappear.

_____ 2. In the next 100 years, more people will record dying languages.

_____ 3. Red Thunder Cloud wanted future generations to hear Catawba.

_____ 4. People liked the songs that Red Thunder Cloud sang.

_____ 5. Languages may die when people move away from their native lands.

_____ 6. The death of a language is a loss for the whole world.

D Relating Reading to Personal Experience

Discuss these questions with your classmates.

1. What are some features that make your native language different from all other languages?

2. Which songs in your language would you record for future generations? Why?

3. What can people do to help save languages that are in danger of disappearing?

Aping Language

Previewing Vocabulary

The words and phrases in the box are from the reading. Discuss their meanings with a partner. Look up any new words in a dictionary.

apes	combine words	communication skills	critics
grammar	linguists	recognize sounds	word order

Scanning

Scan the reading to find and circle the words and phrases from the box. Discuss how you think they relate to the topic of the reading. Then read the whole text.

These are among the things Kanzi, a bonobo chimp, can do: When he hears "give the dog a shot," he grabs a syringe[1] from objects on the floor, pulls off the cap and injects his stuffed toy dog. He understands the difference between "take the potato outdoors" and "go outdoors and get the potato," and between "put the water in the raisins" and "put the raisins in the water." Kanzi also combines words, using shapes called lexigrams, in the correct order. For example, "grab Matata," means that the chimp Matata was grabbed, and "Matata bite" means that Matata did the biting.

1

---

[1] *syringe:* a tube and needle used for putting medicine into the body

2   Impressive, yes. But does that mean Kanzi can use true language? For many years, linguists have distinguished between communication skills like Kanzi's and true language used by humans. Using language requires the use of word order to communicate meaning, as in the raisins-and-water phrases. Sue Savage-Rumbaugh, who directed the research on Kanzi and other chimps, believes that apes are capable of grammar as complex as that used by human two-year-olds. However, her opinion is by no means shared by all researchers. Many of them don't believe that a chimp's ability to understand and use language is anywhere near as complex as a two-year-old child's.

3   Results from studies at the Mount Sinai School of Medicine may help resolve the argument. Researcher Patrick Gannon and his colleagues examined the brains of chimps that had died natural deaths in zoos or labs. They were looking for patterns of activity similar to those that produce language in humans. The researchers found a structure in the chimps' brains, called the planum temporale (PT). Human brains have a similar structure, which is used to understand and produce language. The PT is located in a part of the brain that receives sounds and attaches meaning to them. In 17 of 18 chimps, the PT was larger on the left side of the brain than the right. That is also the pattern in most people.

4   If further research proves that chimps are communicating with the same parts of the brain that humans use for language, it will be hard to argue that chimps do not have some sort of language. However, this theory has many critics. Psychologist Steven Pinker and others believe that the PT in chimps might simply be processing and recognizing sounds – activities that are clearly not on the same level as human language. As scientists continue to do research, the question of whether apes have true language remains highly controversial.

Adapted from *Newsweek*

A Comprehension Check

Every paragraph in the reading is about one topic. Write the correct paragraph number for each topic.

_____ a. a discussion about what true language ability is

_____ b. the findings of research on the brains of dead chimps

_____ c. the sentences that Kanzi understands

_____ d. scientists' disagreement about whether chimps use true language

B Vocabulary Study

Find the words in *italics* in the reading. Then match the words with their meanings.

_____ 1. *grabs* (par. 1)   a. having the ability

_____ 2. *injects* (par. 1)   b. not at all

_____ 3. *capable* (par. 2)   c. end a problem or difficulty

_____ 4. *by no means* (par. 2)   d. gives a shot to

_____ 5. *resolve* (par. 3)   e. a regular way of doing something

_____ 6. *pattern* (par. 3)   f. takes hold of something suddenly

C Paraphrasing

> Paraphrasing a text means using your own words to say what you have read. This is one strategy you can use to improve your understanding of a text.

Circle the letter of the best paraphrase for each statement from the reading.

1. *Using language requires the use of word order to communicate meaning . . .* (par. 2)
   a. Putting words in order is necessary in all languages.
   b. If you don't put words in the correct order, your sentences won't be meaningful.

2. *. . . apes are capable of grammar as complex as that used by human two-year-olds.* (par. 2)
   a. An ape can speak as well as or better than a child at the age of 2.
   b. An ape can understand grammar that is at the same level of difficulty as a two-year old's grammar.

3. *. . . it will be hard to argue that chimps do not have some sort of language.* (par. 4)
   a. People will never agree about the communication of chimps.
   b. Most people will have to agree that chimp communication is a kind of language.

4. *. . . the question of whether apes have true language remains highly controversial.* (par. 4)
   a. There is still a lot of disagreement about whether the language of apes is real language.
   b. We still don't know if the language of apes is real language.

D Relating Reading to Personal Experience

Discuss these questions with your classmates.

1. Do you think the kind of research discussed in the article is important? Why or why not?

2. Would you like to be able to communicate with animals? Why or why not?

3. If animals could talk to people, what do you think they would say? Why?

The Bilingual Brain

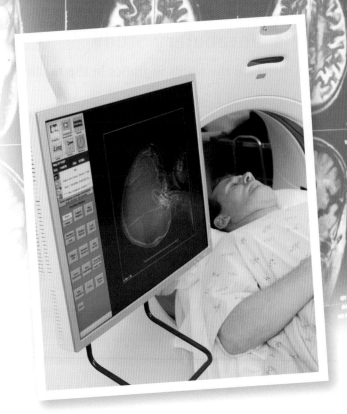

Thinking About What You Know

How much do you know about how people learn a second language? Work with a partner. First, look at the title and discuss the meaning of the word *bilingual*. Then check (✓) the statements you think are true.

_____ 1. It is not possible for an adult to learn to speak a second language fluently.

_____ 2. Children and adults learn a second language in different ways.

_____ 3. Researchers can learn a lot about language learning from studies of bilinguals.

_____ 4. We use special parts of the brain for language learning.

_____ 5. Mothers often teach their babies to speak by using touch, sound, and sight.

Skimming

Skim the reading to find which statements are true according to the writer. Then read the whole text.

1   When Karl Kim immigrated to the United States from Korea as a teenager, he had a hard time learning English. Now he speaks it fluently, and he had a unique opportunity to see how our brains adapt to a second language. As a graduate student, Kim worked in the lab of Joy Hirsch, a neuroscientist in New York. Their work led to an important discovery. They found evidence that children and adults don't use the same parts of the brain when they learn a second language.

2   The researchers used an instrument called an MRI (magnetic resonance imaging) scanner to study the brains of two groups of bilingual people. One group consisted of

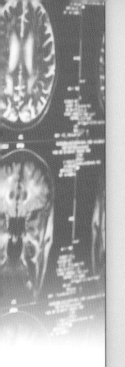

those who had learned a second language as children. The other consisted of people who, like Kim, learned their second language later in life. People from both groups were placed inside the MRI scanner. This allowed Kim and Hirsch to see which parts of the brain were getting more blood and were more active. They asked people from both groups to think about what they had done the day before, first in one language and then the other. They couldn't speak out loud because any movement would disrupt the scanning.

Kim and Hirsch looked specifically at two language centers in the brain – Broca's area, 3 which is believed to control speech production, and Wernicke's area, which is thought to process meaning. Kim and Hirsch found that both groups of people used the same part of Wernicke's area no matter what language they were speaking. But their use of Broca's area was different.

People who learned a second language as children used the same region in Broca's 4 area for both their first and second languages. People who learned a second language later in life used a different part of Broca's area for their second language. How does Hirsch explain this difference? Hirsch believes that when language is first being programmed in young children, their brains may mix the sounds and structures of all languages in the same area. Once that programming is complete, the processing of a new language must be taken over by a different part of the brain.

A second possibility is simply that we may acquire languages differently as children 5 than we do as adults. Hirsch thinks that mothers teach a baby to speak by using different methods involving touch, sound, and sight. And that is very different from learning a language in a high school or college class.

Adapted from *Discover*

A Comprehension Check

Correct the mistake in each statement. The first one is marked for you.

1. Karl Kim was a ~~high school~~ *graduate* student in the lab of Joy Hirsch.

2. Karl Kim learned English when he was a child.

3. In her study, Hirsch used people who speak one language.

4. In the study, both groups of people had learned a second language as children.

5. Inside the MRI scanner, one group was asked to think in one language and then the other language.

6. The scientists looked at one language center of the brain.

7. People who learned a second language as adults used the same area in Broca's area for their first and second languages.

8. The study showed that children and adults use the same parts of the brain to learn a second language.

B Vocabulary Study

Find the words and phrases in *italics* in the reading. Then circle the letters of the correct meanings.

1. *immigrated to* (par. 1)
   a. moved to
   b. left
   c. stayed in

2. *adapt* (par. 1)
   a. create a new situation
   b. change to fit a new situation
   c. add on

3. *consisted of* (par. 2)
   a. talked to
   b. looked like
   c. was made up of, contained

4. *programmed in* (par. 4)
   a. learned by
   b. studied by
   c. read by

5. *taken over* (par. 4)
   a. moved to a different part of
   b. controlled by
   c. thought about

6. *acquire* (par. 5)
   a. read
   b. hear
   c. learn

C Understanding Pronoun Reference

> Writers use different kinds of pronouns to refer to information that is stated earlier in a text. Some common pronouns are *it, they, this, that,* and *those.* Understanding pronoun reference is very important for reading comprehension.

What do these pronouns refer to? Write the correct word or phrase.

1. *it* (par. 1, line 2) _____

2. *they* (par. 1, line 6) _____

3. *those* (par. 2, line 2) _____

4. *This* (par. 2, line 5) _____

5. *They* (par. 2, line 6) _____

6. *They* (par. 2, line 7) _____

7. *they* (par. 3, line 4) _____

8. *that* (par. 5, line 3) _____

D Relating Reading to Personal Experience

Discuss these questions with your classmates.

1. Is it important to know more than one language? Why or why not?

2. What is the best way for teenagers and adults to learn a second language? Why do you think so?

3. If you could learn another language, which one would you choose? Why?

> Reread one of the unit readings and time yourself. Note your reading speed in the chart on page 124.

UNIT 12 The Senses

Look at the titles of the readings and their brief descriptions to preview this unit's content. Before you begin each reading, answer the questions about it.

Reading 1 — Ice Cream Tester Has Sweet Job

What is it like to have a job that requires tasting ice cream all day? In this newspaper article, the writer talks about her interview with one such lucky person.

1. How often do you eat ice cream? What is your favorite flavor?

2. What kinds of things do you think taste-testers look for when they sample food to judge its quality?

3. If you were a taste-tester, what would you like to test all day long?

Reading 2 — Primer on Smell

This article from the Internet answers some frequently asked questions about people's sense of smell.

1. Do you have a good, average, or poor sense of smell? What odors are you good at smelling?

2. Why is it important to have a good sense of smell?

3. Why do you think do some people have a better sense of smell than others?

Reading 3 — How Deafness Makes It Easier to Hear

Surprisingly, some people who are deaf or hearing-impaired can create music. This newspaper article discusses the relationship between hearing loss and musical ability.

1. Who was Beethoven? What do you know about him?

2. What abilities does a composer need to create music?

3. What are some things that help deaf people communicate?

Ice Cream Tester Has Sweet Job

Predicting

The reading is about an ice cream taste-tester. Check (✓) the questions you think the reading will answer. Compare your answers with a partner.

_____ 1. What ice cream company does he work for?

_____ 2. How much money does he earn?

_____ 3. How many samples of ice cream does he taste on a typical day?

_____ 4. What is his favorite ice cream flavor?

_____ 5. What is the most popular ice cream flavor in the United States?

Skimming

Skim the reading to check your predictions. Then read the whole text.

1   John Harrison has what must be the most wanted job in the United States. He's the official taster for Edy's Grand Ice Cream, one of the nation's best-selling brands. Harrison's taste buds are insured for $1 million. He gets to sample 60 ice creams a day at Edy's headquarters in Oakland, California. And when he isn't doing that, he travels, buying Edy's in supermarkets all over the country so that he can check for perfect appearance, texture, and flavor.

After I interviewed Harrison, I realized that the life of an ice cream taster isn't all Cookies 'n' Cream – a flavor that he invented, by the way. No, it's extremely hard work, which requires discipline and selflessness. 2

For one thing, he doesn't swallow on the job. Like a coffee taster, Harrison spits. Using a gold spoon to avoid "off" flavors, he takes a small bite and moves it around in his mouth to introduce it to all 9,000 or so taste buds. Next he smack-smack-smacks his lips to get some air into the sample. Then he breathes in gently to bring the aroma up through the back of his nose. Each step helps Harrison evaluate whether the ice cream has a good balance of dairy, sweetness, and added ingredients – the three-flavor components of ice cream. Then, even if the ice cream tastes heavenly, he puts it into a trash can. A full stomach makes it impossible to judge the quality of the flavors. 3

During the workweek, Harrison told me that he has to make other sacrifices, too: no onions, garlic, or spicy food, and no caffeine. Caffeine will block the taste buds, he says, so his breakfast is a cup of herbal tea. This is a small price to pay for what he calls the world's best job. 4

Harrison's family has been in the ice cream business in one way or another for four generations, so Harrison has spent his entire life with it. However, he has never lost his love for its cold, creamy sweetness. He even orders ice cream in restaurants for dessert. On these occasions, he does swallow, and he eats about a quart (.95 liters) each week. By comparison, the average person in the United States eats 23.2 quarts (21.96 liters) of ice cream and other frozen dairy products each year. 5

Edy's ice cream is available in dozens of flavors. So what flavor does the best-trained ice-cream taster in the country prefer? Vanilla! In fact, vanilla is the best-selling variety in the United States. However, you should never call it plain vanilla. "It's a very complex flavor," Harrison says. 6

Adapted from *The Times-Picayune*

A Comprehension Check

What are the *dos* and *don'ts* of ice-cream tasting? Complete the chart with information from the box.

drink coffee	spit out the sample
drink herbal tea	swallow the ice cream
eat a lot before tasting	taste a small amount
eat onions, garlic, or spicy food	use a gold spoon

Do . . .	Don't . . .

B Vocabulary Study

Cross out the word in each row that doesn't belong to the category in bold. Look back at the reading for help if necessary.

1. **words for judging food:**   avoid   sample   check

2. **words for tasting food:**   order   smack lips   take a bite

3. **parts of the body needed for tasting:**   nose   stomach   taste buds

4. **types of food:**   caffeine   garlic   onion

5. **types of flavor:**   spicy   creamy   sweet

6. **parts of something:**   brands   components   ingredients

C Understanding the Order of Events

> Understanding the order of events in a reading means that you know what happens first, second, third, and so on. This information helps you understand the ideas in the reading.

How does John Harrison taste ice cream? Number the statements from *1* (first step) to *6* (last step). The first one is marked for you.

_____ a. He takes a spoonful of a small amount of ice cream.

_____ b. He opens and closes his lips to add air.

_____ c. He puts the ice cream into a trash can.

_____ d. He takes a breath of air.

__1__ e. He takes out a gold spoon.

_____ f. He moves the ice cream all over the inside of his mouth.

D Relating Reading to Personal Experience

Discuss these questions with your classmates.

1. Do you agree that Harrison has the best job in the world? Why or why not?

2. Would you be a good taste-tester? Why or why not?

3. How would you describe the best meal you've ever eaten? The worst meal?

Primer on Smell

Thinking About What You Know

How much do you know about smell? Mark each statement *T* (true) or *F* (false). Compare your answers with a partner.

_____ 1. Odors, or smells, can warn us about trouble.

_____ 2. Sometimes people can have an emotional reaction to a smell.

_____ 3. Humans have a better sense of smell than animals.

_____ 4. People can be trained to improve their sense of smell.

_____ 5. A 20-year-old has a better sense of smell than a 45-year-old.

Skimming

Skim the reading to check your answers. Then read the whole text.

In addition to bringing out the flavor of food, what does the sense of smell do for us?

Smell "gives us information about place, about where we are," says Randall Reed, a 1
Johns Hopkins University professor whose specialty is the sense of smell. And smell tells
us about people. "Whether we realize it or not, we collect a lot of information about who
is around us based on smell," says Reed.

Even at a distance, odors can warn us of trouble – spoiled food, leaking gas, or fire. 2
"It's a great alerter," offers Donald Leopold, a doctor at Johns Hopkins. For example, if
something in the oven is burning, everyone in the house knows it.

With just a simple scent, smell can also evoke very intense emotion. Let's say, for 3
example, that the smell is purple petunias. These flowers have a rich spiciness that no

other petunia has. Now let's imagine that your mother died when you were three, and she used to have a flower garden. You wouldn't need to identify the smell or to have conscious memories of your mother or her garden. You would feel sad as soon as you smelled that spicy odor.

Compared with animals, how well do people detect smells?

4   That depends on what you mean by "how well." We are low on receptor cells: current estimates say that humans have roughly five million smell-receptor cells, about as many as a mouse. A rat has some 10 million, a rabbit 20 million, and a bloodhound[1] 100 million.

5   Reed says that, across species, there is a relatively good correlation between the number of receptor cells and how strong the sense of smell is. "You can hardly find the olfactory bulb in a human brain – it's a pea-sized object. In a mouse, it's a little bigger. It's bean-sized in a rat, about the size of your little finger in a rabbit, and the size of your thumb in a bloodhound."

Does that mean that our sense of smell is not very acute?

6   Not exactly. While we may not have the olfactory range of other creatures, the receptors we do have are as sensitive as those of any animal. We can also think, and we make conscious (and successful) efforts to tell the difference between one smell and another. A trained "nose," such as that of a professional in the perfume business, can name and distinguish about 10,000 odors. Reed says that a perfume expert can sniff a modern scent that has a hundred different odorants in it, go into the lab, and list the ingredients. "In a modest amount of time, he comes back with what to you or me would smell like a perfect imitation of that perfume. It's amazing."

What happens to our sense of smell as we age?

7   Many people continue to have good olfactory function as they get older. That's not the rule, however. Leopold says that smell is generally highest in childhood, stays the same from the teens through the 50s, and drops starting at about 60 for women and 65 for men. "The average 80-year-old is only able to smell things half as well as the average 20-year-old," says Leopold.

---

[1] **bloodhound:** a dog with an unusually good ability to smell things

Adapted from jhu.edu/~jhumag/996web/smell.html

A Comprehension Check

Write the number of the paragraph where you can find the following information.

_____ a. feelings that certain smells can cause

_____ b. the effects of growing older on people's sense of smell

_____ c. the difference in the sense of smell between humans and animals

_____ d. the human ability to tell differences between smells

_____ e. examples of what smells tell us about our surroundings

_____ f. the effects of the number of receptor cells on the sense of smell

_____ g. examples of how smells can be a warning of danger

B Vocabulary Study

Find the words in *italics* in the reading. Then match the words with their meanings.

_____ 1. *alerter* (par. 2)   a. related to the ability to smell

_____ 2. *spoiled* (par. 2)   b. unusual

_____ 3. *evoke* (par. 3)   c. something that warns you of danger

_____ 4. *scent* (par. 3 & 6)   d. a smell, especially a pleasant one

_____ 5. *correlation* (par. 5)   e. smell (*v.*)

_____ 6. *olfactory* (par. 5)   f. no longer good to eat

_____ 7. *sniff* (par. 6)   g. cause (*v.*)

_____ 8. *not the rule* (par. 7)   h. connection

C Organizing Information into a Chart

> Organizing the information in a text can help you see it in a new way and deepen your understanding of the text. One way to do this is to organize the information into a chart.

Write the items in order on the lines.

1. **Smell receptors:** human, rat, bloodhound, rabbit

   __*human*__   _____   _____   _____

   fewest   most

2. **Olfactory function:** child, 80-year-old, 65-year-old, 49-year-old

   _____   _____   _____   _____

   worst   best

3. **Olfactory bulb:** rat, mouse, bloodhound, rabbit

   _____   _____   _____   _____

   smallest   largest

D Relating Reading to Personal Experience

Discuss these questions with your classmates.

1. What is your favorite smell? What smells bother you?

2. What smells do you remember the most from your past?

3. What smells remind you of winter? What about spring, summer, and fall?

How Deafness
Makes It Easier to Hear

Predicting

Look at the title and the picture. Then circle the letter of the word or phrase that you think will make each statement true. Compare your answers with a partner.

1. Beethoven produced his most powerful works _____ he became deaf.
   a. after   b. before

2. Hearing loss _____ the musical ability of musicians who become deaf.
   a. affects   b. does not affect

3. Deaf musicians _____ music in their heads.
   a. hear   b. do not hear

4. Man-made devices _____ help deaf people hear music.
   a. can   b. cannot

Ludwig van Beethoven
(1770–1827)

Skimming

Skim the reading to check your predictions. Then read the whole text.

1   Most people think of Beethoven's hearing loss as an obstacle to composing music. However, he produced his most powerful works in the last decade of his life when he was completely deaf.

2   This is one of the most glorious cases of the triumph of will over adversity,[1] but his biographer, Maynard Solomon, takes a different view. Solomon argues that Beethoven's deafness "heightened his achievement as a composer. In his deaf world Beethoven could experiment, free from the sounds of the outside world, free to create new forms and harmonies."

3   Hearing loss does not seem to affect the musical ability of musicians who become deaf. They continue to "hear" music with as much, or greater, accuracy than if they were actually hearing it being played.

_____

[1] ***triumph of will over adversity:*** the successful overcoming of difficulty through determination

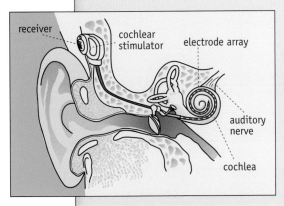

Michael Eagar, who died in 2003, became deaf at the age of 21. He described a fascinating phenomenon that happened within three months: "My former musical experiences began to play back to me. I couldn't differentiate between what I heard and real hearing. After many years, it is still rewarding to listen to these playbacks, to 'hear' music which is new to me and to find many quiet accompaniments for all of my moods." 4

How is it that the world we see, touch, hear, and smell is both "out there" and at the same time *within* us? There is no better example of this connection between external stimulus and internal perception than the cochlear implant.[2] No man-made device could replace the ability to hear. However, it might be possible to use the brain's remarkable power to make sense of the electrical signals the implant produces. 5

When Michael Eagar first "switched on" his cochlear implant, the sounds he heard were not at all clear. Gradually, with much hard work, he began to identify everyday sounds. For example, "The insistent ringing of the telephone became clear almost at once." 6

The primary purpose of the implant is to allow communication with others. When people spoke to Eagar, he heard their voices "coming through like a long-distance telephone call on a poor connection." But when it came to his beloved music, the implant was of no help. When he wanted to appreciate music, Eagar played the piano. He said, "I play the piano as I used to and hear it in my head at the same time. The movement of my fingers and the feel of the keys give added 'clarity' to hearing in my head." 7

Cochlear implants allow the deaf to hear again in a way that is not perfect, but which can change their lives. Still, as Michael Eagar discovered, when it comes to musical harmonies, hearing is irrelevant. Even the most amazing cochlear implants would have been useless to Beethoven as he composed his Ninth Symphony at the end of his life. 8

---

[2] *cochlear implant:* a device, surgically placed in the ear, that changes sounds into electric signals

Adapted from *Sunday Telegraph*

A Comprehension Check

Mark each statement *T* (true) or *F* (false). Then correct the false statements.

_F_ 1. According to Solomon, Beethoven's deafness made it ~~more difficult~~ to experiment when he was composing music.
   easier

____ 2. Three months after becoming deaf, Michael Eagar could hear music in his head.

____ 3. Cochlear implants make it possible for deaf people to hear normally.

____ 4. People with cochlear implants first need to practice using them before they can clearly identify everyday sounds.

____ 5. Cochlear implants help deaf people hear music.

____ 6. A cochlear implant would have helped Beethoven compose more easily.

B Vocabulary Study

Find the words in the reading that match these definitions.

1. this makes it difficult for something to happen   _____ (par. 1)

2. increased   _____ (par. 2)

3. something unusual that happens   _____ (par. 4)

4. show or find differences   _____ (par. 4)

5. satisfying   _____ (par. 4)

6. something that causes activity or a reaction   _____ (par. 5)

7. the quality of being clear and easy to understand   _____ (par. 7)

C Summarizing

> When you summarize a text, you include only the most important information. A summary does not include details or examples. Summarizing is a strategy that can help you check your understanding of a text.

Cross out the three sentences that don't belong in the summary.

Deafness does not affect the ability of musicians to create music because they hear musical sounds in their head. Maynard Solomon wrote about this in his biography of Beethoven. Hearing devices like cochlear implants can help deaf musicians understand what people are saying, but the implants cannot help musicians hear musical sounds in the outside world. In addition, it can take some time to get used to a cochlear implant. Deaf musicians can only hear the musical sound inside themselves. Therefore, a cochlear implant would not have helped Beethoven compose the Ninth Symphony.

D Relating Reading to Personal Experience

Discuss these questions with your classmates.

1. Why might a deaf person *not* want a cochlear implant?

2. What are your favorite sounds in the world outdoors? What are your favorite indoor sounds?

3. What are some examples of successful people who are (or were) either deaf or blind?

> Reread one of the unit readings and time yourself. Note your reading speed in the chart on page 124.

Increasing Your Reading Speed

Good readers understand what they read, and they read at a good speed. Thus, for you to become a fluent reader in English, you need to improve your ability to understand what you are reading; you also need to improve your reading speed.

To do this, you should time yourself when you read a text that is not difficult for you. You may want to read a text several times before you time yourself, or you may want to read the text several times and time yourself after each reading. Both ways will help you improve your reading speed.

The chart on page 124 will help you keep a record of how your reading speed is improving.

After you have completed a unit, time yourself on at least one of the readings. Write down the time when you start reading the text. Then write down the time when you finish reading the text. Calculate the number of minutes and seconds it took you to read the text.

Use the chart below and on pages 122–123 to figure out your reading speed. Divide the number of words in a text by the amount of time it took you to read it. That is your reading speed. For example, if the text is 425 words long and it took you five minutes and 30 seconds to read the text, your reading speed is 77.27 words per minute ($425 \div 5.5 = 77.27$).

As you go through the book, the number of words you can read in a minute should go up. That means your reading fluency is getting better.

Unit	Title of Text	Number of Words in Text	Amount of Time to Read the Text	Reading Speed (wpm=words per minute)
Unit 1 **Names**	What's Your Name?	497 words	_____ minutes & _____ seconds	_____ wpm
	Do People Like Their Names?	421 words	_____ minutes & _____ seconds	_____ wpm
	The Right Name	502 words	_____ minutes & _____ seconds	_____ wpm
Unit 2 **Helping Others**	Don't Just Stand There	516 words	_____ minutes & _____ seconds	_____ wpm
	Random Acts of Kindness	539 words	_____ minutes & _____ seconds	_____ wpm
	Monkey Business	495 words	_____ minutes & _____ seconds	_____ wpm

Unit	Title of Text	Number of Words in Text	Amount of Time to Read the Text	Reading Speed (wpm=words per minute)
Unit 3 Movies	A Dangerous Career in the Movies	435 words	_____ minutes & _____ seconds	_____ wpm
	Life as a Movie Extra	496 words	_____ minutes & _____ seconds	_____ wpm
	The Storyteller	484 words	_____ minutes & _____ seconds	_____ wpm
Unit 4 Families	Living with Mother	501 words	_____ minutes & _____ seconds	_____ wpm
	Father's Day	465 words	_____ minutes & _____ seconds	_____ wpm
	The Sandwich Generation	471 words	_____ minutes & _____ seconds	_____ wpm
Unit 5 Men and Women	The Knight in Shining Armor	502 words	_____ minutes & _____ seconds	_____ wpm
	Men, Women, and TV Sports	456 words	_____ minutes & _____ seconds	_____ wpm
	Boys and Girls in Class	459 words	_____ minutes & _____ seconds	_____ wpm
Unit 6 Communication	Spotting Communication Problems	475 words	_____ minutes & _____ seconds	_____ wpm
	Watch Your Language!	466 words	_____ minutes & _____ seconds	_____ wpm
	What Is Text Messaging Doing to Us?	436 words	_____ minutes & _____ seconds	_____ wpm
Unit 7 Dishonesty	The Telltale Signs of Lying	478 words	_____ minutes & _____ seconds	_____ wpm
	Too Good to Be True	422 words	_____ minutes & _____ seconds	_____ wpm
	Truth or Consequences	496 words	_____ minutes & _____ seconds	_____ wpm

Unit	Title of Text	Number of Words in Text	Amount of Time to Read the Text	Reading Speed (wpm=words per minute)
Unit 8 **Etiquette**	Cell Phone Yakkers Need Manners	440 words	_____ minutes & _____ seconds	_____ wpm
	How Table Manners Became Polite	531 words	_____ minutes & _____ seconds	_____ wpm
	Dinner with My Parents	368 words	_____ minutes & _____ seconds	_____ wpm
Unit 9 **Fear**	Flying? No Fear	560 words	_____ minutes & _____ seconds	_____ wpm
	Don't Fight a Good Fright	467 words	_____ minutes & _____ seconds	_____ wpm
	Stage Fright	451 words	_____ minutes & _____ seconds	_____ wpm
Unit 10 **The Paranormal**	Psychic Solves Crime	413 words	_____ minutes & _____ seconds	_____ wpm
	A Near-Death Experience (NDE)	439 words	_____ minutes & _____ seconds	_____ wpm
	Mind over Matter	537 words	_____ minutes & _____ seconds	_____ wpm
Unit 11 **Languages**	The Day a Language Died	478 words	_____ minutes & _____ seconds	_____ wpm
	Aping Language	411 words	_____ minutes & _____ seconds	_____ wpm
	The Bilingual Brain	408 words	_____ minutes & _____ seconds	_____ wpm
Unit 12 **The Senses**	Ice Cream Tester Has Sweet Job	427 words	_____ minutes & _____ seconds	_____ wpm
	Primer on Smell	523 words	_____ minutes & _____ seconds	_____ wpm
	How Deafness Makes It Easier to Hear	457 words	_____ minutes & _____ seconds	_____ wpm

Reading Speed Progress Chart

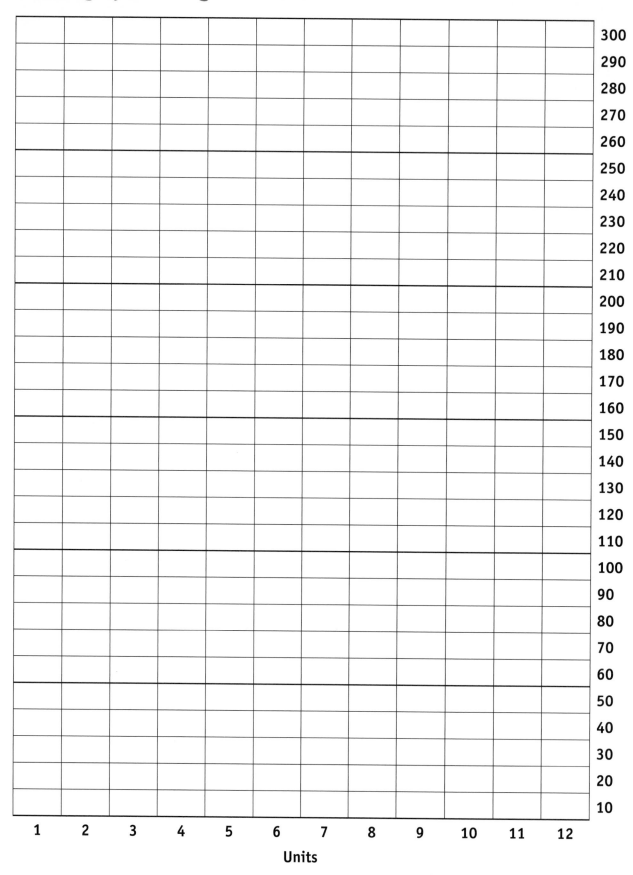

Words per minute

Units

Text and Art Credits

Text Credits

The authors and publishers acknowledge use of the following sources and are grateful for the permissions granted. While every effort has been made, it has not always been possible to identify the sources of all the material used, or to trace all copyright holders. If any omissions are brought to our notice, we will be happy to include the appropriate acknowledgments on reprinting.

2–3   Sources: https://tech.lds.org/forum/showthread.php?3214-Working-with-Names-from-Around-the-World; http://rishida .net/blog/?p=100.

5–6   Adapted from "A sense of identity. Do folks like their first name?" by Mary Lynn Plageman, *The Columbus Dispatch* 4/4/1999. Reprinted with permission from The Columbus Dispatch.

8–9   Sources: http://247wallst.com/2010/10/26/nine-great-brands-that-had-to-change-their-name/2/; http://www.famousnamechanges.net/html/corporate.htm; http://financialedge.investopedia.com/financial-edge/0111/Notable-Company-Name-Changes.aspx; http://www.logoblog.org/wordpress/famous-brand-name-changes/; http://www.salilchaudhary.co.cc/2009/04/story-behind-name-google.html; http://www.pepsico.com.

12–13   Adapted from "If you see someone in trouble, don't just stand there." Copyright © 1993 Condé Nast Publications. All Rights Reserved. Originally published in *Glamour*. Reprinted with permission; adapted from "Why good people don't help" by Harriet Brown. Originally published in the July 1993 issue of *McCall's* magazine. All Rights Reserved.

15–16   Adapted from "Practise Random Kindness and Senseless Acts of Beauty" from the website http://www.globalideasbank.org.

18–19   Adapted from "Guide Dog to Paralyzed Aid Monkey a Saving Grace" by K. C. Baker, *Daily News* 10/10/1998. Copyright © Daily News 1998. Reprinted with permission.

22–23   Sources: http://hubpages.com/hub/How-to-Become-a-Stunt-Person; http://entertainment.howstuffworks.com/stuntmen7.htm.

25–26   Source: http://www.canadianactor.com/actors/extra.html.

28–29   Adapted from "The Storyteller" by Ronald Grover, *Bloomberg Businessweek*, 7/13/1998. Copyright © Bloomberg. Reprinted with permission.

32–33   Adapted from "Living with Mother" by Teresa Poole. *The Independent* 5/27/1994. Copyright © The Independent. Reprinted with permission.

35–36   Adapted from pp. 16–19 *Paper Trail*. Copyright © 1994 by Michael Dorris. Reprinted by permission of HarperCollins Publishers.

38–39   Source: extension.usu.edu/files/publications/publication/FR_Marriage_2006-01pr.pdf.

42–43   Adapted from pp. 138–139 *Men Are from Mars, Women Are from Venus*. Copyright © 1992 by John Gray. Reprinted with permission of HarperCollins Publishers.

45–46   Adapted from "One Game, Two Arenas" by W. Ganz and L. Wenner. *Psychology Today*, September 1992. Copyright © 1992 www.psychologytoday.com.

48–49   Source: http://www.singlesexschools.org/research-learning.htm.

52–53   Adapted from "Tactics for Spotting Communication Problems" by Joanna Cole, *Take Charge Assistant* May 1, 1997, Vol 3. Copyright © 1997 American Management Association. Reprinted with permission.

55–56   Adapted from "Mind your language" by Justin Webster, *The Independent* 3/4/2000. Copyright © The Independent. Reprinted with permission.

58–59   Sources: http://www.associatedcontent.com/article/2477822/text_messaging_is_killing_kids_grammar.html; http://www.bukisa.com/articles/102557_text-messaging-is-it-having-a-negative-impact-on-communication.

62–63   Adapted from "A Fish Story or Not" by Joseph T. Wells, *Journal of Accountancy*, November 2001. Copyright 2001, by the American Institute of Certified Public Accounts, Inc. All Rights Reserved. Reprinted with permission.

65–66   Adapted from "Attributor spells relief when ad claims don't add up" by Anthony Giorgianni, *Minneapolis Star Tribune*, 9/13/1996. Copyright © 1996 Hartford Courant. Reprinted with permission.

68–69   Adapted from "Truth or Consequences" by David Oliver Relin from *The New York Times Upfront*, 1/1/2001. Copyright © 2001 by Scholastic Inc, and The New York Times Company. Reprinted by permission of Scholastic Inc.

72–73   Adapted from "Cellphone yakkers should clam up: People discussing private business in public need lessons in manners" by Patricia Horn, *Philadelphia Inquirer*, 5/8/2000. Reprinted with permission.

75–76   Adapted from "How table manners became polite" by Sharon Huntington, *The Christian Science Monitor*, 11/26/2000. Reprinted with permission of David Huntington LLC.

78–79   From "Four directions" from *The Joy Luck Club* by Amy Tan. Copyright © 1989 by Amy Tan. Used by permission of G. P. Putnam's Sons, a division of Penguin Group (USA) Inc and by permission of the author and the Sandra Dijkstra Literary Agency.

82–83   Adapted from "Flying? No Fear" by Stephen Bleach, *The Sunday Times*, 12/31/2000. Reprinted with permission.

85–86   Adapted from "Don't fight a good fright" by Gary Rotstein, *Pittsburgh Post-Gazette*, 10/31/2000. Copyright © Pittsburgh Post-Gazette, 2011. All Rights Reserved. Reprinted with permission.

88–89   Adapted from "Classical Music; Taking Arms Against Stage Fright" by Eleanor Blau, *The New York Times* 9/20/1998. All rights reserved. Used by permission and protected by the Copyright Laws of the United States. The printing, copying, redistribution, or retransmission of this Content without express written permission is prohibited.

95–96   Adapted from "What is a Near-Death Experience (NDE)?" Copyright 1996–2011 International Association for Near-Death Studies (IANDS). All rights reserved. Reprinted with permission from http://www.iands.org.

98–99   Adapted from "Psychic reveals secrets of her 22 year career cracking crime" by Tim Reid, *The Telegraph*, 6/23/1996. Copyright © Telegraph Media Group Limited, 1996. Reprinted with permission.

98–99   Sources: http://www.unknowncountry.com/news/mind-control-0; http://www.guardian.co.uk/science/2011/apr/17/brain-implant-paralysis-movement; http://www.thekeyboard.org.uk/Telekinesis%20Fact%20or%20fantasy.htm; http://paranormal.about.com/od/telekinesisspsychokinesis/a/aa031703.htm; http://www.mysteriouspeople.com/Nina_Kulagina.htm.

102–103 Adapted from "The day a language died" by Peter Popham, *The Independent*, 1/20/1996. Copyright © The Independent. Reprinted with permission.

105–106 Adapted from "Aping Language" by Sharon Begley, *Newsweek*, 1/19/1998. Copyright © 1998 The Newsweek/Daily Beast Company LLC. All rights reserved. Used by permission and protected by the Copyright Laws of the United States. The printing, copying, redistribution or retransmission of the Material without express written permission is prohibited.

108–109 Adapted from "The Bilingual Brain", *Discover Magazine* October 1997. Reprinted with permission.

112–113 Adapted from "Ice Cream Taste-Tester Has Sweetest Job in America" by Sylvia Rector (Knight Ridder Newspapers), *The Times-Picayune*, 11/9/1998. Reprinted with permission.

115–116 Adapted from "A Primer on Smell" by Elise Hancock, *Johns Hopkins Magazine*, September 1996 issue. Copyright © The Johns Hopkins University. Reprinted with permission.

118–119 Adapted from "How deafness makes it easier to hear in sickness and in health" by Dr. James Le Fanu, *The Telegraph*, 8/11/1996. Copyright © Telegraph Media Group Limited, 1996. Reprinted with permission.

Art Credits

Illustration Credits: 41 Daniel Vasconcellos; 42 Daniel Vasconcellos; 53 William Waltzman; 70 Accurate Art; 119 Adam Hurwitz.

Photo Credits: 1 (t) iMAGINE - Fotolia.com, (c) Comstock/Thinkstock, (b) Vjom - Fotolia.com; 2–3 Tetra Images/Getty Images; 2 iMAGINE - Fotolia.com; 5 (l) Joshua Hodge/AgencyCollection/Getty Images (r) Comstock/Thinkstock; 8 Vjom - Fotolia.com; 11 (t) STOCK4B/Getty Images, (c) Jeffrey Coolidge/Photodisc/Getty Images, (b) Gamma-Rapho/Getty Images; 12–13 tomispin - Fotolia.com; 12 STOCK4B/Getty Images; 15 Jeffrey Coolidge/Photodisc/Getty Images; 17 (tl) I Love Images/Gardening/Alamy, (tc) Exactostock/Superstock, (tr) Jim West/Alamy Images, (bl) Anton Vengo/Superstock, (bc) Terry Vine/Stone/Getty Images, (br) Age Fotostock/Superstock; 18 Gamma-Rapho/Getty Images; 21 (t) neotakezo/www.fotosearch.com, (c) Frederick Florin/AFP/Getty Images, (b) Photos 12/Alamy; 22–23 neotakezo/www.fotosearch.com; 25 Frederick Florin/AFP/Getty Images; 28–29 SSilver - Fotolia.com; 28 Photos 12/Alamy; 31 (t) Jacques Langevin/Sygma/Corbis, (c) Marc Romanelli/Riser/Getty Images, (b) Clarissa Leahy/Riser/Getty Images; 32–33 greio - Fotolia.com; 32 Jacques Langevin/Sygma/Corbis; 35 Marc Romanelli/Riser/Getty Images; 38 Clarissa Leahy/Riser/Getty Images; 41 (t) Ryan McVay/www.fotosearch.com, (b) Jupiterimages/Thinkstock; 45 (l) Ryan McVay/www.fotosearch.com, (r) Fotosearch Silver/www.fotosearch.com; 48–49 George Dolgikh; 48 (r) Jupiterimages/Thinkstock, (l) Gareth Brown/Corbis; 51 (t) Andrew Wakeford/www.fotosearch.com, (c) Gareth Brown/Corbis, (b) Hemera/Thinkstock; 52 Andrew Wakeford/www.fotosearch.com; 55 Gareth Brown/Corbis; 58–59 HaywireMedia - Fotolia.com; 58 Hemera/Thinkstock; 61 (t) Gareth Brown/Corbis, (c) George Doyle/Thinkstock, (b) Corbis/Superstock; 62 Gareth Brown/Corbis; 65 George Doyle/Thinkstock; 68–69 Michael Flippo - Fotolia.com; 68 Corbis/Superstock; 71 (t) Toby Burrows/Digital Vision/Getty Images, (c) David Turnley/Corbis, (b) Buena Vista Pictures/Photofest; 72–73 Patrick Pazzano - Fotolia.com; 72 Toby Burrows/Digital Vision/Getty Images; 75 David Turnley/Corbis; 76 (t) Bananastock/Thinkstock, (b) Dex Image/Getty Images; 78–79 Gabor Takacs - Fotolia.com; 78 Buena Vista Pictures/Photofest; 81 (t) Peter Dazeley/Riser/Getty Images, (c) quavondo/Getty Images, (b) Blend Images/SuperStock; 82–83 Okea - Fotolia.com; 82 Peter Dazeley/Riser/Getty Images; 85 quavondo/Getty Images; 86 (t) Kristen Johansen/Getty Images, (b) Digital Vision/Thinkstock; 88–89 Ferenc Szelpcsenyi - Fotolia.com; 88 Blend Images/SuperStock; 91 (t) Paul Parker/age fotostock, (c) Paul & Lindamarie Ambrose/Getty Images, (b) Mary Evans/John Cutten/The Image Works; 92–93 Paul Parker/age fotostock; 95 Paul & Lindamarie Ambrose/Getty Images; 98 Mary Evans/John Cutten/The Image Works; 101 (t) Associated Press, (c) Anna Clopet/Corbis, (b) Jupiterimages/Thinkstock; 102 Associated Press; 105 Anna Clopet/Corbis; 108–109 svedoliver - Fotolia.com; 108 Jupiterimages/Thinkstock; 111 (t) Washington Post/Getty Images, (c) Medioimages/Thinkstock, (b) Superstock/Superstock; 112–113 Subbotina Anna; 112 Washington Post/Getty Images; 115 Medioimages/Thinkstock; 118 Superstock/Superstock.